BE DIRECT

BE DIRECT

WHY DIRECT RESPONSE MUST
BE AN ARROW IN YOUR
MARKETING QUIVER

Anthony J TaCito

Copyright © 2023 Anthony J TaCito

All rights reserved.

BE DIRECT

Why Direct Response Must Be an Arrow in Your Marketing Quiver

FIRST EDITION

ISBN 978-1-5445-3581-4 Hardcover
 978-1-5445-3580-7 Paperback
 978-1-5445-3579-1 Ebook

For my children,
Sam and Sara Madeleine

CONTENTS

Introduction 1

CHAPTER 1
Customers Are Everything 13

CHAPTER 2
The Difference between Advertising and
Direct Response Marketing 27

CHAPTER 3
The Proliferation of Digital Marketing Channels 43

CHAPTER 4
Direct Mail Is As Relevant As Ever 57

CHAPTER 5
Defining Your Target 71

CHAPTER 6
What Do You Want Them to Do? 83

CHAPTER 7
Presentation of Your Selling Proposition 91

CHAPTER 8
Crafting Your Message 107

CHAPTER 9
ROI—the Goal of Direct Response Marketing 131

CHAPTER 10
Digital Integration: Using Digital Channels
in Direct Response Marketing 141

Conclusion 155

Acknowledgments 163

INTRODUCTION

"I never open any direct mail that comes to my mailbox."

"I toss all my mail in the trash as soon as it arrives."

"No one pays attention to snail mail anymore."

"Direct response/direct mail marketing doesn't work; everything has gone digital."

"It's all just junk mail."

You may have heard some of these types of comments and several others of this nature while sitting in a meeting, debating with team members on how you might best use your company's marketing budget. It's quite possible that you have even thought or said some of these statements yourself. It is understandable, because they're commonly-held notions by many in today's high-tech, digitally powered world.

But these remarks are merely subjective and unfounded statements at best.

Here's how I know: Give me your home or office mailing address. In a few days, a piece of mail will arrive in your mailbox. It will show up as a high-quality envelope that is personally addressed to you. You won't be entirely sure what's inside that envelope, but it will look important.

I'm pretty sure that you will open it, even if only out of curiosity, and even though it goes against your claim that you don't open your mail. You will open it because it looks important, and might have some important information about something that you need to know. I'm willing to bet that upon opening it and once you see that I've sent you a short letter and a $1,000 check made out to you, that you'll cash that check.

For many business owners and marketing executives today, direct mail is perceived as a dinosaur: Old school, dead, and irrelevant in the modern age. And yet, this common scenario—an experience that you may have had in recent memory—represents successful direct response marketing. Any time that a message arrives in the mailbox and resonates in any way with the recipient, the targeted marketing can be considered successful.

Direct response marketing is a technique designed to elicit a desired response by encouraging prospects to take a specific action. In the above example, I wanted the recipient to open the mail, read the message, and cash the check. I can assure you, if a check for $1,000 was sent to you, you would surely read the message to understand the offer and determine if it was in fact a legitimate offer. In this case, a targeted prospect was sent a targeted message and given instructions to cash the check or "take the necessary action."

Many perceive direct response as synonymous with direct mail, but that's actually incorrect. Direct response marketing is a *method*, not a medium. Mail is just one medium through which direct response may be employed. I have spent the past forty-two years working in direct response marketing specializing in direct mail, so this book will naturally focus on that specific medium. But direct response is used successfully through several other types of media, including TV, radio, infomercials, newspapers, magazines, digital retargeting, digital ads on social media, telemarketing, online news outlets, email, and websites and microsites. Often, savvy marketing professionals will integrate direct response marketing techniques into multiple forms of media being used to reach their customers.

Most marketing directors, executives, and business owners today, however, don't understand how powerful direct response marketing can be and how it can be used for their benefit. I would estimate that 90 percent of the executives I encounter have misconceptions about direct response marketing, which leads them to disregard and make uninformed assumptions about it. There is the belief that it is outdated, or what some ad executives might define as "below the line" advertising and marketing methodology.

But in my forty-two years of marketing experience, direct response is undoubtedly one of the best kept secrets in marketing for any company, product, or service.

Consider the difference in what I could have achieved by sending you that check in the mail versus simply telling you about it in a radio ad, TV ad, newspaper ad, or even a digitally placed ad on Instagram, Facebook or Twitter. By sending it via U.S. Mail, I was able to establish a relationship with you. I sent you a personalized message that arrived in your very own, one and only, mailbox, and upon opening it, you decided to take action—you cashed the check all at the behest of the compelling and relevant marketing message that came directly to you from the sender. If I had sent you a message via email, it's likely you may have never even received it. Because, if you haven't engaged with me or my company previously, my message would likely have been automatically sent to your spam folder. You wouldn't have even had the choice to open the email, receive the information, or complete any intended action.

Direct response marketing via a targeted direct mail message affords one of the few opportunities companies and professionals have today to establish and enrich relationships with their customers in a personal way. With the plethora of electronic messaging, apps, and social media at our fingertips, we live in an overconnected—yet highly disconnected—world. Direct response provides a rare but real bit of personal contact between you and your prospect or existing customer. It's simply more direct, and surely more personalized, than running a television spot or social media ad, or even sending an email. And for many businesses, it's exactly what needs to happen to engage new customers and retain existing ones. It affords a personal touch, much like a wedding invitation or a greeting card does; it touches something more personal, more relevant to the recipient.

Today, Marketing Is about Choices

Ultimately, whether you are a professional marketer, salesperson, business owner, professional, entrepreneur, director of marketing, CEO, or board member, bringing in business to drive sales and revenue forms the crux of your mission. How to do that each day, week, month, quarter, or year might possibly be keeping you up at night.

What's the most effective use of your marketing dollars? What is going to give you the most return on your spend and get you the best results? What is going to best represent your brand?

It is challenging to know exactly where to place your advertising and marketing dollars. It can be risky. Your job could be on the line. Your business could be at stake. You could lose it all if you make the wrong decision. Once your money is spent, it's spent.

If you're like many businesses today, you've tried the latest digital technologies currently dominating the marketing landscape, such as social media, retargeting, pay per click, email, and SEO. You've listened to the experts—because it is the conventional modern and up-to-date sexy solution—and there's no denying the digital marketing resources today are broad in scope and seem to be relevant in this age of high tech possibilities. But, it must be recognized that these platforms can be susceptible to bugs, algorithms, and bots, and it's no secret that customers are drowning in digital impressions. And because of that, you might not be seeing the ROI you'd like to realize from using those methods. You aren't acquiring as many new customers as you would like to see, nor are you retaining as many existing ones as you would expect. And you might not be developing long-lasting, rich relationships with your customers.

Especially with digital, it could be that you don't always know what you are truly getting for your spend. Confusion, uncertainty, and doubt abound. How can you continue to make decisions about how to spend your marketing budget when you don't have the necessary data to support what's working and getting you the results you expect? Do clicks really convert to new business? Do views or impressions sell your products and/or service? Sure, Silicon Valley will provide you with charts and graphs, but it is common knowledge that the numbers are not always totally accurate, nor are they representative of what actually is happening with your prospects or customers.

These questions should be in your mind when you review your current marketing strategies. Wouldn't it be nice to have a way to measure your success? To be in touch with what's happening and to know exactly how your marketing dollars are working for you with every marketing spend?

Perhaps it's time to consider the idea that digital isn't the only marketing game out there; that you're ready to try and supplement digital with an omnichannel approach; try something different; find an effective method for reaching your niche target market; to finally see an impressive ROI and measurable results. Studies indicate that consumers are more likely to engage with a company that they have encountered offline and locally. The bottom line is this: direct marketing does work. It works because it can be characterized as a precisely targeted message directed to a precisely targeted recipient who has the highest proclivity to take the desired action at a precisely targeted point in time when the prospect is potentially in the market for the product or service you are selling. It is nothing more than that. In the market, prospects who are in the market for what it is you are selling will respond to messages personally directed to them with a solution to their current problem. Direct response marketing can be best described as salesmanship in print.

Informed Decision-Making Starts with Understanding

This book will provide you with a comprehensive analysis and study of direct response marketing. It will dispel common misconceptions about this powerful approach and show you how it can be harnessed to acquire and keep customers for your business. Every chapter will provide new insights that will give you pathways to extend your brand, your product, or your service to the right customers in a personal way that will enrich the company-customer relationship.

We will discuss the difference between direct response marketing and advertising, and where direct response fits into the current media spectrum. We will examine how direct response marketing provides more targeted, personalized impressions with your customers compared to, for example, TV ads, or wide market placements of ads on radio, internet, newspaper, or on the side of a bus or a highway billboard, allowing your dollar to go further because your targeted message goes to exactly the people you want to get it.

You'll be prompted to think about how to issue a call to action to your target market. What's the most effective use of your ad dollars to draw customers into your business? Do you want them to call you? Maybe you want them to go to your website. Do you want them to come to your place of business and try out your product or services? Place an order for your product or service? Request more information? Set an appointment? Get a free consultation? The response pathways are many.

You will learn how to craft your marketing message to reach your consumers and solicit your desired response. Small details can make a big impact when it comes to piquing prospects' interest, including everything from presentation and format to, most importantly, the content of your message. We'll discuss planning a direct response campaign to fit your budget; timing your campaign for optimal results; how to integrate direct response in the digital world; and how to mine data to understand who to target, how to identify which prospects have the highest proclivity to respond, learn which prospects responded, what did or didn't work for you, and how to leverage those findings to maximize your ROI. That's one of the true benefits of direct response marketing: it's measurable and trackable. You can measure the success of your campaign and leverage that information to make important decisions about how and where to spend your marketing dollars in the future.

Bottom line: by reading this book, you'll gain an in-depth understanding of why, how, and when direct response marketing principles apply to your business. Upon completion, you'll feel motivated to put these ideas to work, to implement, test, and measure direct response techniques, and move beyond lackluster ROI to drive your business's growth higher than it's ever been before.

Learning and Sharing, Based on Experience

I don't proclaim to be the quintessential expert on direct response marketing. I do not profess to be a marketing guru or even a direct marketing guru. I am, however, a perpetual student in the art and science of this fascinating technique of marketing that has brought my clients and my company a great deal of success over the past forty-two years.

In this book, I offer to you the lessons I've learned from producing literally billions of pieces of direct mail and executing more than fifty-two thousand direct response marketing campaigns for more than three thousand clients nationwide. This book is for entrepreneurs who are seeking to start or grow their business. I write for both large and small business owners and retailers, and for professionals who want to build their practices. The jewels in this book can be realized by sales managers, ad managers, marketing managers, ad agency executives, fundraisers, and CEOs. I've heard countless skeptics argue, "Direct response doesn't work." If that statement were true, I would not have been in business this long, or my account management team must have proved to be the greatest salesforce in the world selling a product and service for forty-two years that does not work.

Many marketers I've worked with over the years have expounded the claim, "I don't respond to direct mail." I answer them with an analogy to help them get clear on this medium:

When I go fishing, I put a worm on the end of my hook. The fish goes for the worm, and I catch it, because fish like worms. Now, I don't like worms, I don't eat worms. But I sure like the fish I catch with them!

And so it is with direct mail and direct response marketing. The fish, or the marketplace, likes worms, or direct mail. It works!

Direct response marketing's effectiveness can be largely attributed to its adaptability. The technique is just as effective today as it was more than one hundred years ago when companies sold products via U.S. Mail to rural America because it's a moving target. It's constantly changing as business, marketing, customers, and society evolve. I liken my practice of this marketing method and medium to the practice of a physician. They often don't know the definitive answer to something, but they just keep working at it, practicing constantly, and seeking more knowledge, acquiring current information, and developing a better methodology.

I certainly don't profess to have all the answers when it comes to direct response marketing. I would advise caution when encountering anyone who claims to know it all. But I do have evidence-backed insights that I intend to share with you in the pages of this book.

Join the Conversation

This book is going to give you the basic information you need to know about direct response marketing that will enable you to make informed decisions about why and how this method could and should fit into your marketing plan.

It will give you a well-versed approach and an understanding of something that you may have inadvertently overlooked.

It won't be a panacea, a cure-all, or a how-to. It's not a textbook or step-by-step guide about how to implement direct response marketing. Instead, it's a conversation—and an invitation to consider the possibilities of targeted messaging to targeted prospects.

INTRODUCTION

It's an invitation to ask insightful, fundamental questions about direct response marketing methods and practices, how they can be used and applied, how to measure and track success, and how to offer the elements necessary to consider in order to be successful in the art and science of Direct Response.

I can't give you all of the answers, but I can encourage you to ask the right questions that could boost your company's marketing efforts to launch customer attainment and retention levels to new heights.

I'll even offer up the first fundamental question to ask and continue asking as you embark on this new marketing journey: *What if?*

Direct response is about learning as you go. It's about trying, testing, tracking, and mining data to understand what works best for your business. Continuing to ask, *What if?* has been my secret to success for the past four-plus decades. Now it's your turn—ask yourself, *What if?* What if your company tried something new? What if you have disregarded direct response marketing and it could actually be the solution you've been searching for?

What if you used direct response marketing to connect with more of the people who are the ultimate lifeline of your business's success—your customers?

CHAPTER 1

CUSTOMERS ARE EVERYTHING

"First, you gotta get 'em in the tent."

—P. T. BARNUM

You can't sell or service anyone if
they don't show up or let you know they are
in the market for what you or
your business is selling.

CUSTOMERS ARE EVERYTHING

Years ago, I agreed to rent out a vacant office in the commercial office space I was leasing to a new business owner. Let's call her Debbie. She was the building manager's daughter and she needed a small office space until she got on her feet. Debbie had just opened a medical transcription business, and so she set up her office in the small, open office space that was adjacent to mine. I remember poking my head into her new office a few days after she moved in and being very impressed. She had all the bells and whistles for a thriving business—a new desk and chair, lamps, a copy machine, a phone, a large file cabinet, brand new computer, desk accessories, picture of her daughter, and even supplies such as stapler, sticky notes, and paper clips. It contained everything you'd need for the hustle and bustle of a busy office workday.

There was just one missing piece: she had no customers.

For weeks, the office sat mostly dark and empty. Weeks turned into months, and eventually, Debbie could no longer afford to rent the space from me. She ended up electing to sell her brand-new office equipment and vacate the office while she figured out what was going to be her next venture.

Whether you are a one-person operation, like Debbie's transcription business, or the marketing director for a Fortune 500 company, there is one simple, common truth: *customers are the lifeblood of any business.*

You can have the nicest building, the most competent employees, and the best product or service, but without a steady flow of new and repeat customers, your business will not survive.

Without Customers There Simply Is No Business

A lot of business people don't think about customers as the lifeblood of their business. They lose sight of this fact because they're so wrapped up in doing the day-to-day tasks of their jobs. In my business, for example, team members are performing market analysis, data analysis, creative design, copywriting, account sales and service, project management, accounting, high speed laser printing, and mailshop services. It's easy to forget that we're doing all this for the customer when we're all so focused on doing our jobs. When we're engulfed in each of our roles, the big picture diminishes. But without the orders from our clients that require those tasks to be performed, we would not have a need for all those team members.

The thirty-thousand-foot view is that customers are what drive businesses. I often have to remind my employees that their paycheck comes from our customers. Not the company. It sounds obvious and basic. But we forget that it is because of our customers that we are in business at all. Without customers, there is no business. There is no company. Just like Debbie.

I'm reminding you now because that's the basic premise of understanding exactly what direct response marketing can do for you. It reaches your customers, both existing customers and prospective clients, and allows you to stay connected by communicating with them in a personalized way so you can keep your business relationship with them surviving and thriving for years to come.

Retaining Existing Customers: Maintaining the Relationship

It's important to remember that a customer is only your customer when they're interacting in some way with your business—whether they are on the phone with you, on your website, emailing you, texting with you, reading your brochure, seeing your offer, or responding to your offer by presenting themselves at your place of business, in your store, on your showroom, at your office, or at your restaurant. The minute they disconnect with you or your business either virtually or live and in person, there's a chance that they may never come back. There is always a worthy competitor whispering in your customer's ear, making claims that they can do what you do better than you, cheaper than you, quicker than you, and all with the promise of providing a more pleasant experience, yielding higher quality, better performance, improved value, greater satisfaction, exceptional results, etc.

This makes it critical for you to stay in touch with your customers. It's like maintaining a relationship. If you never talk to your spouse, for example, you can't expect your marriage to continue to do well. It's the same when retaining customers—you must constantly keep your flow of communication to keep your customers engaged with you and keep your business top of mind.

It's worth it to put in the effort to maintain these relationships. It's well known that a repeat customer is twice as likely to buy as a first-time buyer. A big reason for this is people are creatures of habit. If you go to a retail store of any kind and have a good experience, you're more likely to go back because you're familiar with that store. You know how to get there and where to park. You know your way around the store displays. You know the employees. It's more comfortable than trying a new store because you know what to expect.

With this philosophy, it's easier and more efficient to retain customers than continue to gain new ones. Business success depends on customers coming back again and again. Repeat customers, steady revenue flow. Business schools call it organic growth.

How can you capitalize on the business from repeat customers? Direct response marketing campaigns are among the most effective strategies for maintaining ongoing relationships with customers that result in customer retention.

Imagine a customer visits your store or business, or calls your office for the first time and has a positive experience, but they have yet to take the next step in your sales funnel. You might mail them a letter, or possibly an invitation to make an appointment, or you could offer 20 percent off their next purchase if they bring the letter to your place of business.

Now let's dissect how that message works for you to maintain and retain the existing customer relationship:

It's personalized. The letter is addressed to the customer and has their name on it. It wasn't sent to everyone, and they know this because it's timed to coincide with when they're due for the product or service you sell—i.e., an oil change, winterizing their home, a new roof, siding, plumbing, eye exam, or dental appointment. Because the message has the prospect's name on the marketing (by the way, the most important word to anyone is their name), their name now becomes associated with you, your business, and your product or service. Seeing one's name in print is compelling, and causes one to relate to or associate with the printed word.

Your targeted message creates top of mind awareness, or TOMA. TOMA is critical to building your brand and strengthening customer relationships by always keeping your business and your brand on your customer's mind. When they think of a business that provides your product or service, they think of your brand over all others because of your constant communication.

It elicits action. To build upon that awareness, your letter invites your customer to do something—make an appointment and/or bring in the letter for a discount or a special offer that is realized only with this marketing message. This seeking of action is what sets direct response marketing apart from other types of advertising and makes it so effective for continuing to bring customers into your business.

The action is measurable. You'll know if your campaign worked if the customer made an appointment and presented the marketing as you asked them to do. It's simple to track, as well as justify, the use of your marketing dollars because the action you elicit from the customer is measurable. Further, you can continue to communicate in the way that works to prompt those customers to continually return.

It keeps the customer *your* customer. Each time a second (and beyond)-time customer comes into your establishment with your marketing message in hand, they are once again your customer. The consistent, personalized communication you provide through direct response marketing is one sure way you can maintain that relationship for successful customer retention.

Gaining New Customers: A FREE Offer

Similarly, direct response marketing allows you to attract both old and new customers in creative and personalized ways. One of the best ways? *Offer a free gift or a free offer of some value.*

Offering free gifts is one of the most effective marketing strategies you can employ to cultivate new customer relationships. Consider any one of a multitude of items to offer as a Free Gift for visiting or shopping with you—a cooler, a pen set, a tote bag, an umbrella, cookware, a gift card, a tool set, a first-time service, or hundreds more—whatever it is, "free" is the most valuable word you can use in any direct response marketing piece.

Consider, for example, a direct response marketing campaign for a car dealership. The dealership sends invitations to prospects inviting them to visit the dealership to attend a four-hour sale, where discounts will be in effect for four hours only, and just for attending the event, the prospects will receive a free set of steak knives. Customers begin streaming into the dealership, presenting the invitation in exchange for a set of steak knives.

It seems straightforward—and completely unrelated to selling cars. But take a closer look at this scenario.

The potential customer hands the salesman the invitation, and thus the salesman surely hands them the free gift. Meanwhile, they strike up a conversation.

Because the invitation says that they will get a free gift for attending the special event, and because the salesperson does exactly that (handing the prospect a free gift), all the other claims and offers being made about the sale event become believable as well. I've witnessed thousands of prospects come to a dealership seeking a free gift, and an hour later, leave the dealership driving home in a brand-new car.

"Which model of new car or truck are you interested in buying today?" the salesman asks.

Sometimes the prospect responds with, "I don't think I am ready to buy a car today. I just wanted to come by, see the deals, look at a few cars, maybe take a test drive, and pick up my steak knives."

A novice or unprofessional salesperson or marketing professional could get discouraged. You might be led to believe you have wasted your dollars on a premium offer, and it didn't immediately lead to a sale. But here's what's really happening: The potential customer got up off their sofa, left their home, letter in hand, and made their way to the dealership. That's quite a lot of effort on their part, and it creates several benefits and opportunities:

It creates the opportunity to gain a new customer, just by that person entering the business. Perhaps they *do* want to buy a car that day. They can't become a customer of the dealership if they don't ever enter the establishment or become engaged in a way that allows a sales professional to make a presentation to them that might ultimately lead to the prospect making the purchase. Anyone who responds to an invitation similar to this voluntarily puts themselves into this vulnerable position to be sold something. A seasoned sales professional understands this dynamic. There is exceptional value to the fact that the customer responds to the invitation, thereby placing the salesperson in control of the sales process.

Even if the customer doesn't make a purchase that day, it helps establish a relationship with that prospective customer. The salesman continues making friendly conversation with the potential customer and gets to know them. The salesman might learn that the potential customer can't buy a car today because they're out of a job and don't have the money for a down payment. But they've been dutifully job hunting and hope to be employed soon. In the meantime, they'll mention this dealership to their neighbors down the street, both of whom the potential customer knows will be in need of a new car soon.

It forms a habit. Drawing the potential customer into the dealership aids them in creating a habit that will enhance their likelihood of doing business with you in the future. When they do have the money and the time comes when they do need a new vehicle, they're more likely to come to the dealer with whom they're familiar, comfortable, and have had a positive interaction where they have been in the store. They know their way to the dealership, where to park, where the front door is, and what the showroom feels like. They have even made a "friend" there, the salesperson who gave them a free steak knife set, no questions asked.

It enhances credibility. By offering a gift to the potential customer and following through on that offer, you reinforce the validity of everything else in the letter about your business. You promised a free gift and you delivered on that promise. So when you send another direct response piece offering 20 percent off a purchase, the customer can trust they will actually receive that price discount. Ultimately, this builds trust in your business, which is a huge qualifier for obtaining and retaining customers.

It opens the door for the rule of reciprocation. This is the idea that, by giving this potential customer a free gift, they may feel obligated to give you a shot when the time comes to purchase a vehicle.

Ultimately, offering the free gift allowed the dealership to create a rich relationship with a real customer that can then be maintained and nurtured. The potential customer and the car salesman exchange contact information that day, and three months later, the salesman calls the customer to follow up.

"I just wanted to see how things are going for you," says the salesman. "Any luck with the job search?"

Perhaps that customer has, in fact, found a job, and they are ready for a new vehicle. The two set up a time for the customer to come in and discuss their options.

A customer has been gained, a relationship established—and it all stemmed from a direct response marketing piece offering a free gift.

The Impact of an Invitation to Draw in Customers

I experienced the power of direct response marketing through mailed invitations and free gift offers firsthand when I worked as a regional sales manager for a major automotive manufacturer. We were in the midst of a high-interest-rate period in our economy, a time when some automakers were on the verge of bankruptcy. Dealerships sat full of unsold vehicles. Manufacturers had thousands of newly-made cars that were unsold by dealerships around the country, and they needed help selling them.

Always looking to learn and grow in my marketing tactics as a regional sales manager, I read a book that taught me about mailing offers to people to elicit a response. Suddenly, something inspired me: *what if we sent an invitation to potential car customers inviting them to come to a four-hour sale?* Cars would be specially priced, and customers would get an additional discount above and beyond the special pricing. We'd include a $300 check in the letter, and if they brought that to the sale, they could put it toward their purchase, but it was only good during those four hours. And on top of all that, attendees would also get a free gift. The event was "by invitation only," a private sale, not being held for the general public.

Our invitation felt exclusive, special, personalized, and urgent—this offer was only good for four hours only on the date and time specified! And if you received this letter, you had access to the sale before any other announcement was made to the public. You were able to get a first look at the huge selection of cars and trucks before anyone else, and you were entitled to take advantage of the special discount pricing as an invitation holder.

We rented a large tent and assembled it on local fairgrounds so it could house the thousands of cars we needed to sell. The ten dealerships in the area and all of the sales personnel from each dealership convened at the tent to sell the vehicles.

Our event drew in customers by the thousands.

Within hours of the event, hundreds of vehicles were sold. The manufacturer was relieved of their surplus of cars, and dealers sold cars and gained new customers. Since then, we have conducted thousands of events like this nationwide with a similar response.

This experience launched my career in direct response marketing. If it could work for large tent sales like this, why couldn't it work for each individual dealership? I started working with other dealerships and businesses to develop similar events that would drive retail traffic and to create, design, print, and mail the associated letters and invitations.

That was the moment I knew—this *works*. Direct response marketing has the potential to reach new and existing customers more effectively than any other marketing tactic. It allows for the personalized communication necessary to foster a loyal customer base.

Because the age-old truth remains: customers are everything. Without them, your business cannot survive. It makes connecting with new and existing customers of the utmost importance, and that means targeting them in the most efficient and effective way possible. How do you choose the best method to do that? The first step is understanding the difference between direct response marketing and what you're probably doing in at least some capacity right now: advertising.

CHAPTER 2

THE DIFFERENCE BETWEEN ADVERTISING AND DIRECT RESPONSE MARKETING

"Smart is stupid, stupid is smart."

We often overthink things and get in the way of the simple solution.

THE DIFFERENCE BETWEEN ADVERTISING AND DIRECT RESPONSE MARKETING

Oftentimes, we know too much and it gets in the way of what the customer really wants, or wants to know. Therefore it is best to keep quiet, ask intelligent questions, and direct your presentation around what information the prospect or customer is seeking.

Advertising is mostly Brand Building. The word brand might not be the first thing you think of when you hear the word now, but for a long time, the concept of branding was associated with one thing: cattle.

For centuries, livestock were branded with their owner's mark so that cattle ranchers could easily identify their cows in a pasture. Even today, the concept of brand advertising is not much different than that. If you continue to see Bob's Brand everywhere, you will likely become aware of the magnitude of the stock held by Bob. Advertising keeps your company's name, product, or service in the mind's eye in the marketplace, with the sole purpose of building consumer awareness and associating your brand with the product or service you provide.

But it's important to remember that advertising as a marketing method is a broad brushstroke and only one part of the entire marketing mix. While you could ultimately reach prospects seeking your product or service, you will also reach *other* consumers who might not be in the market for what you're offering; and that's OK, but you are paying to reach all those other people who might not have any interest at all in you, your company, your product, or your service.

Even the most experienced marketing professionals may view direct response marketing and advertising as one and the same, but that's wholly inaccurate and can be detrimental when making decisions such as where to spend marketing dollars. Often, the smartest path is the simplest, and it's right in front of us.

Direct response marketing delivers everything advertising does, but it allows you to disseminate your message in a much more targeted and personalized approach. Rather than spending money reaching customers who don't fit within your target, you can focus your efforts only on those who have the proclivity to do business with you or buy your product or service. Direct response marketing also extends your efforts one step beyond traditional advertising by involving a call to action, which pulls your prospects directly into the sales funnel. With a response request built in, your prospect voluntarily engages with you and your brand. Response tracking allows you to measure the effectiveness of your lead generation and ultimately you have the ability to calculate a Return On your Invested Ad Dollars (ROAD or more commonly known as ROI).

Now think about your current marketing strategy: is a large percentage of your marketing budget spent painting with a broad brushstroke to boost brand awareness? Could it be more targeted? More measurable? More precise? If the answer to any of these questions is yes, it's worth understanding how direct response marketing and advertising compare, and how you might complement that broad brushstroke with a more targeted approach that could be reaching prospective customers in a more efficient way.

Advertising Is about Brand Awareness

Let's start with a little Marketing 101. At its root, advertising is just one form of marketing and it is meant to tell a brand's story and increase its visibility. It spreads the word in a large-scale, general way to a wider audience using numerous public forms—digital, Facebook, YouTube, Instagram, Twitter, TV, radio, newspapers, magazines, billboards, point of purchase, and much more.

Often, advertising pulls on emotions. Think of the ads you see during the Super Bowl: some are funny, others heartfelt, some downright strange. It's all meant to do one thing: imprint a brand on your brain; to make it so the next time you're in need of the product or service the brand offers, you remember that commercial, how clever it was, and choose that brand because of it. That's advertising at work.

As a side note, next Super Bowl, pay attention to the ads. In 2023, the ads cost $7 million for a thirty-second spot. That does not include the actors, production, film, editing, music, and other costs necessary to get your attention. Then, the day following the Super Bowl, see how many of those ads you can remember, much less the name of the company, the product or service they were advertising, and most importantly, what was their offer? What was it they wanted you to do? Did they give you a call to action? Did they give you a reason to shop? A reason to buy? Did you buy what they advertised? Did they establish a personal relationship with you? Did you engage with the advertiser as a result of the ad?

Advertising puts a brand on customers' radar. It stimulates interest and gets their attention. It might even create some desire. But there's one important takeaway: advertising does not yet sell. Advertising does create desire; it can grab attention, and it oftentimes even creates interest. But that is where advertising stops and where direct response picks up. Direct response differs in that it urges the prospect or customer to take action, and additionally, it provides the means to do it. Direct response provides an order form, coupon, phone number, email address, website, QR code, or special response mechanism that will get the prospect to take action, at that very moment, then and there. Direct response takes the offer, the opportunity, the deal, the value—right to the customer.

An advertisement ends when the entertainment or artistic value is presented. It rarely elicits a measurable action from the customer, so there is no way of knowing if the advertisement had a direct result in the form of a prospect or a sale. Advertising also doesn't necessarily always reach *just* the right people who would make a purchase. Just as it could reach prospects who are the best target, it is likely that it also reaches people who would never do business with you, simply because they are not the highest and best prospects for your product or service.

And that's OK. Brand advertising isn't *necessarily supposed* to sell or create the measurable results seen with direct response. It's supposed to be used to spread the word widely and reach many people with your brand's message. Brand advertising likely belongs in your marketing strategy. The problem is that, often, it's given too much authority—too much spend—and it's expected to bring in sales when that's not its purpose. As a result, many companies end up spending big on brand advertising and not benefiting with an ROI they want or expect.

To reach the right people, make the sale, and attain a satisfactory ROI, you need a method that's more targeted and measurable. This is where direct response marketing takes center stage.

Direct Response Marketing Extends Beyond Advertising

Direct response marketing does everything advertising does and much more. It extends beyond a brand advertisement by including one critical element: a call to action to the customer. An advertisement often quits after the brand message, leaving the customer with the task of recalling the brand, the product, or the service, who must then take action on his/her own volition without any incentive other than their own emotion to drive the action. Direct response marketing communicates the brand message and then elicits a specific, measurable response that brings the customer into your sales funnel.

This is the key difference between direct response marketing and advertising: direct response invites the prospect to do something —"Bring this coupon in for 10 percent off," "Come in for a free quote," "Join us for an exclusive event on this date," "Text this code to take advantage of this two-for-one offer," "Call for a free estimate," "Call or email for an appointment." It initiates a relationship with the customer, and allows your customer to have a pathway to do business with you. Direct response marketing gets prospective customers *in the door* of your business, which in turn increases the likelihood that they'll engage with your company and/or make a purchase.

To clarify, direct response can be accomplished using any type of media. Anytime you issue a call to action to the customer, you're employing the concept of direct response marketing. The lack of a response mechanism is what distinguishes an advertisement from a direct response.

Admittedly, methods like direct mail are among the most effective for executing direct response. I've never seen someone bring a TV under their arm into a business because a nonresponsive ad prompted them to make a purchase. I have, on the other hand, time and time again seen customers bring in a coupon or a private invitation that they received in the mail and I've seen thousands of customers respond to a Call Now # across a TV screen for a multitude of consumer products and services.

Direct Response Focuses Your Targeting

Direct response marketing also allows you to target your message in a much more focused way to the exact prospect that you are seeking who meets the criteria you are looking for. Imagine you own a swimming pool cleaning service. You can knock on every door in a neighborhood asking if they'd like to purchase your service. But only five of the twenty houses you visit even have a swimming pool. Think of the time, energy, and money wasted on the houses that didn't have a need for your service. If those were dollars instead of time and footsteps, you would have wasted money and time.

THE DIFFERENCE BETWEEN ADVERTISING AND DIRECT RESPONSE MARKETING

Visiting every house in the neighborhood can be compared to brand advertising—it's a blanket marketing strategy that's much less tailored to fit each home's specific needs, but it does get your brand message out widely.

To focus your efforts and increase your chances of making a sale, you might take the time before you launch on a solicitation journey to locate all the houses with swimming pools and only visit those houses. You might even uncover all the people who have month-to-month pool cleaning contracts or contracts that will be expiring soon. There are several drill downs you could perform to narrow your focus and only target the prospects who might actually buy from you. Then, you make them your offer—a reason to connect with you and your company instead of their current provider, or even if they don't have service, a reason why they should have your company servicing their pool. That's the art and science of direct response marketing. It's identifying the people with swimming pools and then spending your money to reach them because they are the best prospects for your business. It's sending a targeted message to a prospect that you best believe will resonate with your message, based on factors such as demographics, psychographics, proximity, buying habits, income, need, etc. and then asking for a measurable response to bring those entities into the sales funnel.

Sometimes, the brand advertising method you are using simply doesn't effectively reach your target market. You devote several months' worth of your marketing budget to an ineffective ad medium. Because of sunk costs, you continue to spend in that arena and then you wait and hope to see its effectiveness. Unfortunately, you will have spent thousands of dollars trying to reach an audience that is just one fragment of the market who buys, needs, or wants what you offer. And, more than likely, you probably won't know for sure what ad it was that piqued their interest unless you make a concerted effort to determine what it was that brought them to you.

Contrast this with sending a discount coupon to the correct targeted prospect in the form of a letter, invitation, flyer, or postcard. It reads, "Make an appointment and bring this with you for a FREE [X]." You send it only to individuals who fall within the demographics of your targeted clientele—prospects in the identified age range, who live in the geographical market area you serve. You don't waste your time or money reaching people you know are very unlikely to have an interest in or want, need, or buy your product or service, even after they've seen your messaging.

You also personalize the message to speak directly to each prospect letting them know what you know about them, their lifestyle, their needs, their problems, their fears, their desires, etc.

In this case, you can see how a direct response marketing approach is a more effective use of your money than just brand advertising alone, because you can target your prospective customers more accurately. You're not sending a blanket message out to the masses. It's focused, targeted, and personalized to your exact prospective customers.

Urgency Creates Value

Direct response marketing is also one of the best ways to capitalize on one of the most powerful concepts in marketing: fear of missing out, or FOMO.

If you choose direct mail sent through the United States Postal Service (USPS) as the direct response medium you use to reach prospective clients, you should also include a sense of urgency, such as a limited time offer, or "this offer expires on [X date]."

Suddenly, you've elevated your message's importance in the customer's eyes; you've added urgency, which enhances value and creates more impetus to get an immediate response. You've instigated the customer's FOMO and urged them to act soon, within the timeframe you want. By placing this urgency into the response vehicle, with a specific time to respond, it allows you to visibly see the effects of your campaign. Once recipients begin to respond to your offer during the established dates and times, a measurable spike in traffic, internet leads, texts, phone calls, and sales revenue can be observed.

This immediate call to action establishes an increased level of control that's unfound in advertising. You control what you want your customer to do and when you want them to do it.

Measurability and Budget Control

Budget Flexibility and the measurability of your ROI are two additional elements of control you can realize with direct response marketing that are more difficult to achieve with general brand advertising. They are arguably the most important distinction between these two methods.

Simply put, you have a far greater ability to tailor a direct response marketing strategy to your budget, especially using direct mail and email. However, digital advertising, and even TV advertising, can be regulated according to your budget more easily than most other advertising media. Depending on the medium, advertising spend is often a function of what the media provider sells or packages for you and your campaign. Television ads and billboards, for example, have set costs associated with them; you either pay for it or you don't run the ad. With direct response and direct mail in particular, if your budget only allows you to send ten pieces of communication in a month, you can still send those ten pieces to the most valuable prospects you can identify. Or, if your budget allows, you can send fifty thousand pieces. It's completely tailored to your strategy and budget.

With a drip style budget, you do have the ability to measure ROI simply and quickly. Not all marketing and advertising methods give you quantifiable results that provide absolute clarity on the effectiveness of your strategy. It's difficult to clearly attribute most forms of advertising media directly to a customer sale.

But with direct response marketing, you absolutely, positively know the source of your lead or prospect and that they reached out to you because of your direct marketing communication. If your prospect or customer presents a printed offer in the form of a letter, invitation, postcard, or flat that you sent to them while positively responding to whatever action you requested, there's a direct correlation. You know that your direct response communication was effective and thus you can accurately calculate ROI.

Here's an example. You're a car dealer who mailed ten thousand letters inviting customers to a sale on a certain date between 1:00 p.m.

THE DIFFERENCE BETWEEN ADVERTISING AND DIRECT RESPONSE MARKETING

and 5:00 p.m. Of the ten thousand invitees, one hundred and twenty-five people came into the dealership, letter in hand. You know this because you greeted each customer at the door. Out of those customers, thirty-five bought cars, all with an average price point of $45,000. You spent $10,000 on your mailings, but you made $500,000 in gross sales, of which you made about $50,000 in profit. Therefore, you know your ROI was five times what you spent on your direct response marketing communication. It is not unusual for us to see results as high as 200% to 10,000% return on an investment with a direct response marketing campaign.

Similarly, when your TV ad airs, you'll likely get some numbers related to how many people tuned into the programming during that time, and it is often not concrete data. There's no telling how many people actually watched your ad. As a result, calculating exact ROI becomes challenging. Better would be a direct response TV ad, much like what you see in the form of an infomercial with a call now phone number. The best example of this is the My Pillow Guy who begs you to "call now." This is classic direct response advertising utilizing the medium of television broadcasting. Many of you might remember the K-tel ads, selling oldies, or the TV ads selling the Flex Seal waterproof materials, weight loss programs, sleep aids, and many, many more. Those are all classic direct response ads. Each one asks you for your order—*call now*!

When you're a marketing director formulating the best strategy for your business, there's no greater insight than that—the ability to measure and attribute the actual ROI in an intelligent and scientific way, and to understand what works and what doesn't so you can put your dollars to use most effectively and efficiently. Best of all, these formats are not static. You have the ability to adjust your offers, your budgets, your targets, all as a result of your close monitoring of your response metrics.

Direct Response Marketing vs. Digital Advertising

You might be thinking: what about digital? What about social? You might be wrestling with social media, retargeting, SEO, and PPC all the while trying to decide where, among the myriad digital marketing channels available, you should put your money. Compared to other advertising platforms, digital marketing does offer somewhat similar benefits in the way of targeting and tracking. And while much of our discussion is centered on direct mail because that's where my forty-two-year career expertise lies, I am also a strong advocate for integrating and combining your digital marketing strategy and your direct response marketing strategy as a powerful one-two punch. We'll dive deeper into how to do that later in this book.

Digital marketing is no doubt effective for many marketers in some scenarios, but when used as an advertising method, it still can be a much broader brushstroke compared to the precise approach of direct response. The digital marketing space is inundated with options, channels, methods, formulas, and messages. Quite frankly, both marketers and consumers alike are overloaded with information, and are disconnected in a vastly connected world. In fact, this massive proliferation is the biggest obstacle to successfully employing digital as the one and only piece of your marketing strategy, and it warrants a deeper discussion. We will get to it.

CHAPTER 3

THE PROLIFERATION OF DIGITAL MARKETING CHANNELS

"Simplicity is the ultimate sophistication."
—LEONARDO DA VINCI

The best advice is to keep it simple.

THE PROLIFERATION OF DIGITAL MARKETING CHANNELS

Many people tell me that they don't open their direct mail, or it's just not for them. That's OK with me. But I have to explain, with forty-two years of experience seeing with my own eyes lines of people responding to a direct mail campaign, I know that the people who are interested in the product or service you are selling at the time, and who are in the market, undisputedly respond with vigor.

"When a tree falls in the forest and no one hears it, does it make a sound?"

You have likely heard this philosophical question before and may have considered the ambiguity of the answer. Now equate that to a question you might ask yourself or your team at your next marketing strategy meeting: "When a marketing email gets sent out, does it land in the spam folder or the recipient's inbox, and further, does it get read, and do we know if in fact it does make a sale? To be fair, some marketers are sophisticated enough to have the metrics that follow and track the effectiveness of their email marketing efforts. They might know open rates and click through rates, and possibly even conversion rates. I would be very impressed if they were able to measure sales revenue, profit, and ROI from their email campaigns.

Unlike a philosophical puzzle, you can't afford an ambiguous response with your marketing budget on the line. In fact, when it comes to digital marketing, email is one medium that can be termed an unpredictable method because any email you send to a prospective customer who you don't already have a relationship with will most likely end up in their spam folder. Just look at your email spam folder right now and think of all the marketing dollars that were spent for email messages that went directly to your spam folder, unseen by the intended recipient—you. These issues of reach and ROI extend beyond email. In fact, as much as 60 percent of digital marketing is fraudulent and fails to get your message in front of an actual human prospect.

Knowing this, how do you effectively deploy digital marketing and its multitude of options?

The truth is, it's not about email. Or Facebook. Or social media. It's about response. Without a response mechanism, all of these digital platforms still fall under the scope of brand advertising; the broad brushstroke that creates brand awareness but doesn't definitively bring customers in to make a purchase.

When used wisely, the digital marketing channels available today are powerful. They're the way of the future, and the future is now, and most companies must and should incorporate digital as part of their marketing strategy. Yet, digital channels are of limited value when used alone or solely as advertising vehicles. These conventional digital platforms could be greatly enhanced and become much more efficient when employed as part of direct response marketing campaigns. Fail to consider this added benefit, and you could be missing an opportunity to optimally reach your target market and maximize your ROI.

Digital Marketing's Proliferation Problem

Before we can even consider how to most effectively use digital marketing with direct response, we must first get a handle on the mind-boggling amount of digital marketing channels available today. In any given month, you might be weighing options such as banner ads, Twitter, Facebook retargeting ads, Instagram, Pinterest, TikTok, email blasts, SEO, and pay-per-click, to name just a few.

As the executive in charge of marketing and sales, where do you even start? How do you spend your money? Where do you spend it, among the many, many options available? What's going to cut through the excess and allow you to actually grow your customer base, drive more sales, increase revenue, and make a profit?

As a perpetual student of marketing, I am continuously amazed by the plethora of information available on digital marketing. Marketers are currently spending as much as 50 to 90 percent of their marketing budgets on digital advertising. Experts everywhere have recommendations and lengthy commentary on data algorithm technology, predictive analytics, touch points, retargeting, SEO, SEM, SMS, and on and on. There are such concepts as propensity to buy scores, Google AdWords, "Google's Quality Score" of paid search, the efficacy of CRM for social media, search engine results pages (SERPs), keywords, metatags, impressions, clicks, average position, and conversions, just to name a few.

As a CEO, CIO, CMO, or marketer, you can study digital attribution, content production, search volume, and search intent, and, of course, there is more information that you should be familiar with, such as the high-value pages on your website and search results pages. There are several SEO tactics that are very important to consider, such as page speed, reduced bounce rates on your website, and increased opportunities for conversions. You might find yourself immersed in analyzing Search Console data totaling millions of queries, seeking out more insight into short tail queries and intent qualifiers.

Tired? If you aren't tired yet, I haven't mentioned site metadata and content, and relevant landing pages. You need to know that you must be creating content around longtail searches where prospects are seeking in-depth information about you, your company, your products, or your service. Since by now you might have a good grasp of your Google Quality Score (QS), you should be able to calculate your ad rank. That now brings us to topics like what you pay, or your bid price for paid search, PPC, SEM, or whatever you choose.

Whichever your method, you have to bolster your QS to qualify. The key is relevance. The QS influences important metrics like click to call, geolocation, call-outs, message, site link and structure snippets. And, it is imperative that you do not miss the importance of pushing customers or prospects "below the fold" on their mobile device when you are properly executing this strategy.

To me, this is head spinning. It is a digital treadmill, and direct response allows you to jump off of it. How in the world can you be knowledgeable about all of this BS unless you have a BA, BS, MS, MBA, MFA, and a Ph.D. from MIT?

THE PROLIFERATION OF DIGITAL MARKETING CHANNELS

There's no doubt that the promise of this technology is exciting. It's "sexy." You've been hearing it for years: any successful company today *must* have a strong digital presence.

Compared to other media like broadcast or cable TV, OTT, newspaper, radio, point of purchase, Text, or billboards, digital options like Facebook, Instagram, Twitter, and others, do offer improved targeting thanks to today's algorithms that tailor ads based on a user's online activity. I can perform a quick Google search of my next vacation destination and the next time I log into Facebook, I'm sure to see ads related to my search.

Some customers may view this as intrusive. It's also not uncommon for these algorithms to misfire or be off track. Still, digital is getting closer and closer to the precise targeting that's achievable with direct response marketing via mail.

The problem with digital compared to a medium like direct mail is proliferation.

Customers are bombarded with digital messages and images. It's estimated that most Americans are exposed to between four thousand and ten thousand ads each day, distributed over a variety of platforms. Of all the touchpoints in a shopper's journey, the marketer risks introducing the shopper to the marketer's competitors. So, all of that digital spend just brings the shopper closer to somewhere you don't want them to go.

Comparing digital advertising proliferation to direct mail, could you imagine what the acceptance rate would be for direct mail if there were four to ten thousand pieces of mail in your home mailbox each day? There is no doubt, you might have a different view of the effectiveness of mail. That said, why is it acceptable to have four to ten thousand digital messages fired at you all day long, and it is somehow accepted? Marketers are laying down for the digital spend regardless. They might consider this simple analogy.

And while the average customer might have thousands of digital ads hidden away in their iPhone, their postal mailbox is their one and only postal mailbox. This is the place where the prospect or customer will not be introduced to your competition. Your competition does not have the opportunity to influence your customer when your customer opens your targeted message. There's also nobody there sifting through the mail, taking out the items deemed as irrelevant and unuseful. Because the United States government guarantees it, your mail message gets delivered. What happens to it after that is up to the recipient.

In this way, direct mail remains to be still more targeted and highly visible and tactile to recipients. The direct mail gets into the home when the salesperson just can't. Some say that there is less mail being delivered right now due to all this digital brouhaha. Well, that's good for you. Less overall mail in the mailbox means that your message is more impactful, and even more relevant. Surely nothing close to four thousand per day!

Digital's ROI Impact Is Unclear

In today's digital world, it's true that you can tell who clicked on a Facebook ad and where they went afterward—to your website, for example. What you often can't do, however, is completely attribute a sale of your product or service to that Facebook ad. It makes attribution in digital marketing confusing and misleading, and measuring direct ROI from a digital marketing campaign extremely difficult.

Digital marketers will tell you the opposite of this as part of their sales pitch. They will credit a sale to a Facebook ad just because the consumer visited your website after clicking on the ad. But the customer may have also visited ten other sites before they went back to your site and decided to make a purchase. They may have seen twenty-five other ads on other digital platforms that influenced that buying decision.

I can tell this lighthearted but relatable story to illustrate:

You go out on a Friday night for some drinks with friends. You start off at Joe's Bar and have two beers. Your friends suggest you go to Sam's Saloon down the street, and you have two more beers there. Then, you decide to head across the street to Tony's Pub, where you have a margarita. You end the evening with a nightcap at Jenn's Cocktail Lounge.

On the walk home, you realize you're feeling pretty buzzed. Was it the nightcap that got you buzzed? Or was it an accumulation of all you drank? It's the latter, of course. And it's the same with Facebook and other forms of digital ads. In most cases, we can't definitively attribute a sale or a lead to one single ad, just like we can't blame your eventual morning headache on your nightcap at Jenn's.

The online customer's journey is winding and complex, and we can't be 100 percent certain the ad was the reason a consumer bought, *unless you include a call to action.* Direct response marketing allows for total attribution because you know exactly who you targeted and if they acted on your response mechanism, whether that's bringing in a letter, calling, texting, clicking on your exact response button, scanning a QR code, or going to your website to register, get a free gift, request a quote, a consultation, an appointment, or a percentage off a purchase price.

Research supports the point that measuring ROI is difficult to accomplish with digital marketing. Researcher and consultant Augustine Fou identified marketing professionals' feedback about the effectiveness of digital advertising as "hand-wavey-ness" and "wishy-washy." "They assume that digital marketing works because sales are happening," Fou wrote. "But they cannot say [it] concretely. Saying that some 'brand favorability or recall' metric went up is not concrete. Sales were happening anyway, whether digital ad spending was occurring or not."

Fou even found that when several large companies, including Procter & Gamble, Chase, and Uber, cut millions of dollars in digital advertising, it made no difference in their sales outcomes. Experiments with other clients showed similar results.

When a pharmaceutical company, for example, turned off one of their digital advertising platforms, it cut traffic to the company's site in half. One would hypothesize that the lost traffic would be accompanied with a loss of conversions. But this was not the case. Conversions did *not* decrease with the decrease in traffic, revealing one unfortunate truth: much of the company's website traffic could not be attributed to legitimate visitors with functioning eyes. Instead, they were likely bots, software programs designed to perform automated tasks that mimic or replace human behavior. Bots are useful in instances such as performing customer service tasks or indexing search engines. They cannot, however, become your customer.

Unfortunately, this pharmaceutical company is not alone—digital advertising spend lost to fraud is in the tens of billions globally. Facebook has reported canceling billions of fake accounts. When your business is a victim of digital ad fraud, clicks become about as useful as unread spam emails—they have no chance of leading to sales.

Direct Response Opportunity Can Be Found in Digital Marketing

Clearly, I am not a digital advertising expert. Far from it. However, my experience situates me well to tell you how direct response marketing works in and in conjunction with digital marketing. We will take a closer look at how exactly to integrate digital marketing and direct response in Chapter 10, but for now, I'll offer these two ideas:

Direct response can and should be used in digital marketing. I said it before and I'll say it again: brand advertising—including ads on digital platforms—likely belongs in your marketing strategy. But when allocating your budget, *you can't expect brand advertising to sell.* You need a call to action to do that.

There are ways to include a response mechanism in a digital advertisement, whether it's a banner ad or social media post. "Call this number," "Go to this website," and "Click here" are all ways to utilize direct responses digitally. Truly, the principles of direct response can be applied to every marketing medium available.

Other methods of direct response marketing should be used alongside digital advertising, including direct mail. We know it's important to have a strong digital presence in today's business world, but no successful company focuses its marketing efforts solely online. Diversification is key.

I'll give you an example. I received a piece of mail at my office with a message that read: "Right now, people are looking for businesses just like yours. Make sure Tacito Direct shows up the moment potential customers search for what you have to offer—whether they're at home or on the go." It continued on about how consumers today want quick answers to their questions and how valuable it is to be visible to the internet-searching public.

The targeted direct mail I received was sent to me, a business owner, and was from Google. That's right. You read right, Google!

I've received several similar letters from other tech giants, including LinkedIn and Verizon. Even the most high tech businesses pair their digital advertising efforts with methods such as direct response mail to accurately and precisely target prospective customers. If you are like me, you have probably received hundreds of direct mail letters and interesting packages from companies with brands you well know, such as Chase Bank, Bank of America, American Express, AT&T, Spectrum, AAA, State Farm Insurance, Visa, Mastercard, and many, many more, just to name a few. You cannot convince me that these "Captains of Industry" in boardrooms across the country are not wisely considering every option when they choose to spend millions on mail.

THE PROLIFERATION OF DIGITAL MARKETING CHANNELS

When you send an email, your email provider decides if it gets into your inbox. When you send a letter, it gets to your mailbox, period; the United States government guarantees it. Some still argue that mail gets thrown away. But it's your targeted prospect who makes that decision. If they opt to throw it away because they're not interested, they are presently not in the market for it, or simply don't have the resources to buy what it is that you are selling, they still see your brand and your message. They have complete control over that decision—unlike the decision made for them to not see messages that are sitting in their email spam inbox.

You have complete control, too, over who you target and the content of your message. Amidst the proliferation of digital media channels, direct response mail is often more targeted and direct. It pays to refine and personalize your message to cater to your exact target audience, and there's often no better way to do it than with the perfectly placed, highly targeted direct response marketing message sent through the USPS.

CHAPTER 4

DIRECT MAIL IS AS RELEVANT AS EVER

"Men are moved by two levers only: fear and self."

—NAPOLEON BONAPARTE

People only buy to get benefits.

DIRECT MAIL IS AS RELEVANT AS EVER

I read an article recently with a headline that caught my attention:

"Direct mail is hot again."[1]

The article described how hip, modern companies like Wayfair, Rover, Quip, and Modcloth were targeting millennial customers via direct mail. It described the method as "hot" due to the trust younger consumers have in it—they don't associate direct mail with "junk mail" the way older consumers tend to do. In fact, younger consumers are more likely to associate "junk" with email.

These ideas align with our opening discussion in this book—that direct mail remains a relevant marketing method for companies and marketing professionals today. And while there are many types of media you can leverage to implement direct response marketing, direct mail is one of the most powerful options available. Buying into the false notion that direct mail is ineffective and aged in an increasingly digital environment could be hindering your ability to formulate an optimal marketing strategy for your business.

A snapshot of further research reveals additional eye-opening facts and information that support direct mail's relevance and importance in today's business world, including:

---

[1] Rieva Lesonsky, "Direct Mail Is Hot Again. Here's How to Use It," *SBA Blog*, U.S. Small Business Administration, April 4, 2019, https://www.sba.gov/blog/direct-mail-hot-again-heres-how-use-it.

- 70 percent of consumers prefer traditional mail for cold, unsolicited offers.[2]
- 70 percent of consumers say direct mail is more personal than online interactions.[3]
- 48 percent of people retain direct mail for future reference.[4]
- 86 percent of consumers say that they use coupons that they received in the mail.[5]
- 76 percent of consumers trust direct mail over digital channels when they want to make a purchase decision.[6]
- 42 percent of overall recipients read or at least scan direct mail pieces, meaning you can reach nearly half your intended audience with a mailing.[7]

---

[2] Association of National Advertisers, "ANA/DMA 2018 Response Rate Report: Performance and Cost Metrics Across Direct Media," November 15, 2018, https://www.ana.net/miccontent/show/id/rr-2018-ana-dma-respose-rate.

[3] Matt Mansfield, "Direct Mail Marketing Statistics for Small Businesses," *Small Business Trends*, January 10, 2017, https://smallbiztrends.com/2017/01/direct-mail-marketing-statistics.html.

[4] Craig Smith, "10 Print Marketing Statistics You Should Know," DMR, last updated January 8, 2023, https://expandedramblings.com/index.php/10-print-marketing-statistics-know/.

[5] *2K17 Valassis® Coupon Intelligence Report: Influencing Consumers Along the Path to Purchase* (Valassis, 2017), 6, http://www.199it.com/wp-content/uploads/2017/03/2017-3-21PDF-Coupon-Intelligence-Report.pdf.

[6] Daniel Burstein, "Marketing Chart: Which Advertising Channels Consumers Trust Most and Least When Making Purchases," MarketingSherpa, January 17, 2017, https://www.marketingsherpa.com/article/chart/channels-customers-trust-most-when-purchasing.

[7] Carolyn Goodman, "Is It Old Fashioned If It Still Works?" Wisconsin Direct Marketing Association, February 23, 2018, https://wdma.org/2018/02/23/is-it-old-fashioned-if-it-still-works-carolyn-goodman/.

- ▶ 59 percent of millennial-aged consumers find the information they receive by mail to be more useful than information received via email.[8]
- ▶ 80 to 90 percent of direct mail gets opened compared to email at 20-30 percent.[9]
- ▶ Direct mail campaigns generate purchases five times larger than email campaigns. When you combine the two mediums, it yields purchases six times larger than email alone.[10]

When we dig deeper into the evidence, as we'll do in this chapter, it's quickly apparent that direct mail is not, in fact, dead. There is a myriad of statistics and information about business landscape changes, consumer trends, digital advertising data—and even scientific research—that show just how effective this marketing method and this medium is for most organizations today.

Mail's Revised Role in a Changing Business Landscape

The mistaken perception that mail is dead is rooted in the belief that mail is a slow and inefficient way to reach a customer or prospect whether it's a marketing message, a personal letter, an invitation, or even a thank you note. With email, text messaging, social media messaging, and more, why would you send a letter that takes a day or two

---

[8] United States Postal Service, *Still Relevant: A Look at How Millennials Respond to Direct Mail* (United States Postal Service, 2019), 2, https://www.uspsdelivers.com/wp-content/uploads/A_look_at_how_millennials_respond_to_direct_mail.pdf.

[9] Mansfield, "Direct Mail Marketing Statistics."

[10] Lesonsky, "Direct Mail Is Hot Again."

to arrive when you can send a digital message that arrives instantly? In fact, with electronic banking, bill paying, and Venmo, it does seem somewhat outdated.

But when we take a step back, we can see that direct mail is no longer just a method for sending those messages, letters, postcards, flyers, and notes. Particularly since the Covid pandemic, direct mail has played a revised role in consumers' lives, and as a result, it's not only surviving—it's thriving.

When Covid forced all of us to mostly stay home, mail became a key ingredient in our day-to-day activity. For many of us the postman's daily saunter up to the mailbox was the highlight of the day. Looking forward to what came in the day's mail. It became a habit, for me and for many. Consumers received information about open service businesses and delivery options and even how to interact online with merchants while quarantined. Many of us began to do most of our shopping either online or through the mail. According to the *Harvard Business Review*, catalog mailings had already been rising steadily since 2015, with response rates increasing by 170 percent from 2004 to 2018. Millennials in particular report being interested in the catalogs they receive in the mail.[11]

While pandemic restrictions have lifted and, for most of us, life has returned to a semblance of what it was before, Covid's impact is unforgettable. The changes it caused in both our daily lives and in

---

[11] Jonathan Z. Zhang, "Why Catalogs Are Making a Comeback," *Harvard Business Review*, February 11, 2020, https://hbr.org/2020/02/why-catalogs-are-making-a-comeback?registration=success.

business are here to stay. That means the centrality of mail in consumer life remains—so much so that consumers don't just rely on mail, they are excited about it. One-third of consumers report feeling more excited to receive their mail each day than they were before Covid-19.[12] Seventy-three percent of millennials say they would be upset if they no longer received mail, and 80 percent of millennials look forward to seeing what they receive in the mail.[13]

Eagerness to get the mail combined with more time at home means increased time spent with direct mail marketing pieces, as well. Thirty-four percent of consumers say they are spending more time reading marketing mail than before the pandemic, and 46 percent say they are more interested in obtaining promotions, deals, or coupons than they were pre-pandemic.[14]

Add to this that 88 percent of key purchases for retail, financial, and automotive categories are discussed at home, and we see how the fact that direct mail is sent to an entire household, as opposed to an email sent to one person, is extremely valuable. In fact, direct mail has a seventeen-day shelf life compared to an email's lifespan of just a few seconds. This means mail pieces may linger on kitchen tables, desks, or counters for much longer as customers review and revisit them, increasing exposure to both the content and the likelihood of action.[15]

---

[12] "Using Direct Mail Marketing Strategically during COVID-19," USPS Delivers, accessed April 17, 2023, https://www.uspsdelivers.com/pandemic-marketing-strategy-for-small-businesses.

[13] United States Postal Service, *Still Relevant*, 3.

[14] "Using Direct Mail Marketing Strategically."

[15] Lesonsky, "Direct Mail Is Hot Again."

All of this makes mail more relevant than ever today.

Mail's Effectiveness Versus Digital Platforms

This relevance of mail is in addition to the fact that the medium is significantly more effective than most of its digital counterparts.

The average consumer sees between four thousand and ten thousand digital ads[16] and receives one hundred emails *per day*.[17] Meanwhile, just two to four pieces of direct mail are received per day. Over the past ten years, as digital marketing has increased, direct mail volumes have declined. The USPS reported a marketing mail volume of 66.2 billion pieces in 2021, which was down from a 103.5 billion high in 2007.[18] This gives direct mail more "real estate" in the mailbox—and in a consumer's mind. Less mail received overall bestows more relevance and impact to your message when it arrives.

Data on ROI as well as open, read, and response rates adds more evidence of direct mail's effectiveness.

According to a study from the Direct Marketing Association, direct response marketing using direct mail outperforms all digital

---

[16] Jon Simpson, "Finding Brand Success in the Digital World," Forbes Agency Council, *Forbes*, August 25, 2017, https://www.forbes.com/sites/forbesagencycouncil/2017/08/25/finding-brand-success-in-the-digital-world/?sh=4cbde00a626e.

[17] Stefan Campbell, "How Many Emails Does the Average Person Receive per Day?" *The Small Business Blog*, last updated December 21, 2022, https://thesmallbusinessblog.net/how-many-emails-does-the-average-person-receive-per-day/.

[18] Michael Plummer, "Three Reasons Mailers Aren't Dead in 2022," Forbes Technology Council, *Forbes*, July 14, 2022, https://www.forbes.com/sites/forbestechcouncil/2022/07/14/three-reasons-mailers-arent-dead-in-2022/?sh=16c3535f5c9d.

platforms combined by a whopping 600 percent.[19] What's more, according to the Association of National Advertisers, letter-sized direct mail has the highest average ROI of all marketing media at 112 percent when sent to prospect lists. That's compared to email marketing's average ROI of 93 percent, despite it being the most used marketing medium in 2020, and SMS average ROI of 102 percent.[20]

Further, research reported by the American Marketing Association says direct mail open rates can vary between 57.5 percent and 85 percent—that's three to four times higher than email open rates. Direct mail response rates range from 2.7 percent to 4.4 percent, compared to email's 0.6 percent average response rate.[21]

Direct response marketing via direct mail is also largely viewed as reliable and more trustworthy than digital marketing. While the United States government hand delivers your direct mail message to your potential consumer, 33 percent of millennial consumers use ad blockers, which means that digital ads don't even reach their intended recipient.[22] Fifty-eight percent of millennials say they have

---

[19] Chris Hamlin, "Not Dead Yet: Direct Mail Outperforms Digital Channels by 600%," LinkedIn, August 17, 2015, https://www.linkedin.com/pulse/dead-yet-direct-mail-outperforms-digital-channels-600-hamlin-mba.

[20] SeQuel Response, "Direct Mail ROI Surpasses Digital Mediums," LinkedIn, January 31, 2022, https://www.linkedin.com/pulse/direct-mail-roi-surpasses-digital-mediums-sequel-response?trk=pulse-article_more-articles_related-content-card.

[21] "Direct Mail Campaigns Aren't Dead: 7 Ways to Boost Responses and Save Money," American Marketing Association, October 13, 2022, https://www.ama.org/2022/10/13/direct-mail-campaigns-arent-dead-7-ways-to-boost-responses-and-save-money/.

[22] United States Postal Service, *Still Relevant*, 6.

fewer privacy concerns related to direct mail than they do with digital communications.[23]

It's not just older consumers who may struggle with digital technology that embrace direct response messages sent via direct mail. Consumers from the Baby Boomer generation all the way to Gen Z express a desire and openness to direct mail. Seventy-one percent of Baby Boomers (consumers born between 1946 and 1964) believe mail feels more personal than digital marketing, and 88 percent of Gen X consumers (consumers born between 1965 and 1980) prefer a blend of physical and digital marketing messages. For millennial-aged consumers (those born between 1981 and 1996), 65 percent say they pay attention to mail; 88 percent take time to look through it; and 62 percent say they tend to read through their advertising mail rather than discarding it without reading.[24] Finally, Gen Z consumers (born between 1997 and 2012) say positive customer reviews are a leading reason they buy from specific brands, and direct mail allows for reviews to be displayed and shared in a reliable, trustworthy way.[25]

Regardless of generation, much of the consumer desire to return to physical marketing pieces is due to the digital fatigue that emerged from the pandemic. According to the American Marketing Association, digital fatigue is "a state of mental exhaustion and disengagement

---

[23] "Millennials and Mail: 5 Myths and the Truth Behind Them," USPS Delivers, accessed April 28, 2023, https://www.uspsdelivers.com/millennials-and-mail-5-myths-and-the-truth-behind-them/.

[24] "Using Direct Mail Marketing Strategically."

[25] "Direct Mail Campaigns Aren't Dead."

that occurs when people are required to use multiple digital platforms at work or at home." Simply put, research shows that humans need a break from screens. The digital overwhelm contributes to lowered attention spans and a lack of focus, leaving consumers longing for something tangible and real to read.[26] Additionally, 72 percent of internet users find pop up ads "very annoying" and 49 percent view banner ads to be just as irritating. Direct mail offers a tactile, distraction-free way to reach consumers.[27]

Going Digital with Direct Mail

While the benefits of direct mail as compared to digital are apparent, marketing directors today must consider the best approach to a successful campaign in our increasingly digital world. For many, that's omnichannel marketing. Embracing direct mail doesn't—and shouldn't—mean abandoning digital altogether. For most companies, the most effective direct response marketing plan will include a mix of direct mail and digital channels to achieve the maximum reach and response rates.

Research, once again, supports this claim, thanks to a neuromarketing study conducted by USPS and Temple University. Researchers measured consumer reactions as they recalled digital ads they had

---

[26] "Direct Mail Isn't Dead," *AMA Las Vegas* (blog), accessed April 18, 2023, https://amalasvegas.com/direct-mail-isnt-dead/.

[27] Carolyn Goodman, "Is It Old Fashioned If It Still Works?" Wisconsin Direct Marketing Association, February 23, 2018, https://wdma.org/2018/02/23/is-it-old-fashioned-if-it-still-works-carolyn-goodman/.

viewed on a tablet and physical ads they had viewed on a postcard. The conscious reaction was gauged by asking questions about brand recall, brand association, and brand discrimination. The subconscious reaction was evaluated using eye tracking, core biometrics, and functional magnetic resonance imaging to study brain activity as ads were being viewed. The researchers also compared the effect these ads had on two different age groups of consumers—those aged forty-one and younger, and those forty-seven and older.

Overall, the physical ads were found to leave a more lasting, conscious impression than digital ads across age groups, as consumers had stronger memories of these ads. Subconsciously, both age groups processed the physical ads faster than the digital ads, although the younger consumers processed the physical ads much faster than the older participants.

In the end, the study pointed to the ultimate benefit of combining media for the best marketing strategy, with digital media serving as the fastest way to communicate an idea, gain attention, and deliver a message quickly. Print materials, including catalogs, postcards, and mail pieces, however, produce a higher emotional effect on a consumer, causing a long-lasting impact that results in easier recollection. "The most effective campaigns," the researchers wrote, "will use both in combination to create omnichannel experiences that excite and engage."[28] Today, marketers deploying multichannel

---

[28] "Is Direct Mail Advertising Effective? A Research Study," USPS Delivers, accessed May 10, 2023, https://www.uspsdelivers.com/why-direct-mail-is-more-memorable/.

campaign strategies report using an average of three media types per campaign.[29]

The beauty of direct mail as a medium for direct response marketing is that not only is omnichannel marketing possible, but marketers can also integrate digital responses within their physical mail pieces to elicit the highest response possible. Today, a mailed brochure or letter can urge consumers to visit a website to buy online, or scan a QR code to watch a video or schedule an appointment. Many marketers simply use mail to announce to prospects with the highest proclivity to buy their product or service the existence of a website or microsite, and motivate them to go to preferred web pages where buyers can shop inventory, set an appointment, request information, or actually make a purchase.

When digital interaction can be communicated via mail, it's often far easier for the consumer to act upon. They don't have to remember a number or URL from a TV ad, for example. They don't need a pencil and paper handy to jot down the information they need. They can simply refer back to the printed mail piece they have retained, scan the QR code or visit the website URL, text, or email address. Meanwhile, marketers can reap the benefits—and the ROI—of various marketing media in their strategy to maximize campaign results.

---

[29] SeQuel Response, "Direct Mail ROI Surpasses Digital Mediums."

Direct Mail Is More Relevant Than Ever

As the data shows, now is certainly not the time to start writing a eulogy for direct response marketing. It's alive and well—and remains extremely effective. Some very successful brands have built their business using this method, including Harry and David, Duluth Trading, Chase Bank, Citibank, Abercrombie & Kent, American Express, Visa, Backroads, Sprint, AT&T, L.L. Bean, and Omaha Steaks, along with hundreds more. Even *The New Yorker* magazine solicits subscriptions via mail. They've done so and continue to because it generates the expected results and return on investment. Believe it or not, I have boxes of direct mail I have received from both Google and LinkedIn. Imagine that! A digitally based company using direct mail to reach me, a business owner. Direct response marketing with direct mail is reliable, predictable, and measurable—and in today's world, it's as relevant as ever in helping you to reach real customers and prospects in a very personalized way.

CHAPTER 5

DEFINING YOUR TARGET

"People aren't interested in you, they're interested in themselves."

—DALE CARNEGIE

People are not interested in things,
only what things can
do for them.

Have you ever tried to play a game of darts...blindfolded? It's no surprise that without being able to see your target, you are bound to fail, no matter how good your aim is with full vision.

It's the same with direct response marketing. If you don't know who and where your best potential and existing customers are located, both geographically and metaphorically, your marketing might be misguided. The first step in a direct response marketing initiative is to define your target. It's arguably the most critical component to a successful direct response marketing campaign.

Just like in a blindfolded game of darts, with a sense of direction and some luck, you might be able to get a dart on the board. But without impeccable knowledge and a clear vision of your target, you'll never hit the bullseye.

Use Demographics and Psychographics to Define Target Criteria

When it comes to defining your target, the best source of knowledge is your existing customer base—after all, your customers are already doing business with you. Observing their demographic and psychographic traits can not only help you maintain those relationships but also identify future customers.

You're likely already familiar with the terms *demographic* and *psychographic*. Both demographics and psychographics describe the characteristics of a data set. Age, location of residence, marital status, number of children, and income level are just some examples of the demographic information you may gather about your customers. Meanwhile, psychographic information includes interests, lifestyle, personality, attitudes, beliefs, and values.

Understanding these characteristics allows you to define your current customers, as well as pinpoint your target prospects. Prospects are people who most *look* like your customers, meaning they have similar demographics and psychographics, but they haven't done business with you yet. While existing customer relationships should be a primary focus of your marketing to enhance organic growth, targeting prospects with direct response marketing campaigns will also generate growth for your business.

Holding on to and retaining your customers and maintaining ongoing relationships with your existing customer base is the basic tenet of a business. Keeping your brand top of mind with your existing clients is what will sustain you as you grow your business. Your first and best choice for your direct response messaging is to your existing customer database. This is why it is essential that you have an ongoing CRM or customer database that contains the customer information you need to reach them via USPS, email, and phone.

Purchase history, frequency, market basket size, and product purchases are essential information when targeting your existing customers with direct response messages. You must keep your brand in front of your customers as often as possible and direct response is a very efficient method of maintaining that ongoing personal relationship that sticks customers to you.

I often argue with my automotive dealer clients who tell me that their customers are "their customers." My contention is that, unless they are in the dealership, they are not their customer. Too many dealerships in the marketplace are making a bid for their customers' business. Because of this, a business must be constantly in contact with its existing customer base, and direct mail is, in my opinion, the most effective medium to do that.

Geographic, demographic, and psychographic information will help you set criteria for who to target in your direct response marketing campaigns by categorizing customers and prospects based on this data. Take an example of a car dealership. The dealership's assigned market area is an approximate twenty-five-mile radius around the dealership's location. The market area encompasses six adjacent towns—two in each direction—and six zip codes. Knowing this information, we could identify the following criteria for campaign targets:

1. **Existing customers who reside in the assigned market area zip codes.** Zip codes are the best source of targeting for the dealership because most customers and prospects reside in those areas. One target for a direct response campaign could be existing customers residing in the zip codes of the dealership's assigned market area (the market defined by the franchisor as where the dealer is responsible for sales and service market penetration).

2. **Prospects who reside in the assigned market area zip codes.** In addition, the dealership might also send targeted messages to prospects who reside in those identical zip codes. These prospective customers look like the dealership's customers—they may share matching demographic information, such as age, marital status, income level, buying history, or purchase behavior—but they haven't given the dealership any business yet. Since the message to a current customer should be different from that of a prospective customer, a targeted message sent to prospective customers should be a different campaign offer or message than the one sent to current customers.
3. **Customers who live outside the market area.** Even if a customer lives outside the market area, the dealership must keep in touch to maintain and nurture that existing customer relationship. It's like keeping in touch with an old friend—you need consistent and regular communication to keep the relationship going.
4. **Current drivers of vehicles in and around the market area.** The dealership could identify a fourth group of targets for a direct response marketing campaign—current drivers of vehicles of the same brand the dealer sells who live in and around the market area, but who bought their current vehicle from a different dealership. These prospects look like current customers *and* their likelihood of visiting the dealer for service or to purchase a new car of the same

brand is heightened because those consumers already drive what the dealership is selling. These factors make these consumers a valuable group to target.

This fourth point can be illustrated in another way. When I visit Italy, I buy clothes at an Italian brand retail store. When I'm at home in Dallas, the retail stores in the shopping center near where I live send me direct response marketing mail pieces because I'm a prospect for their business—they sell products similar to what I buy in Italy. My geographic location, demographics and psychographics portray me as a likely prospect of the shopping center near my home; therefore, I'm a valuable prospect worth targeting. This philosophy can be applied to any business when identifying prospects.

Psychographic information about your market helps to further categorize your targets and tailor your messages within the targets you have defined. The dealership would not target a prospect for a Jeep Rubicon in the same way they would target a new parent who might be a good prospect for a minivan. These consumers likely have different interests and values, particularly when it comes to the features in their next vehicle. These differences must be considered when defining your campaign target and deciding the message that will have the most impact.

Mining Your Customer Database

All of this brings us to the next important question: *how does a marketing executive or business owner go about finding this information?* The most valuable resource at your disposal is ideally at your fingertips—your own customer database. The ability to data mine your existing customers is an essential aspect of defining your target in direct response marketing, and its success is a function of how well the data is captured and managed.

A customer database consists of the names of people who have done business with you and contains useful information about the customers—everything from their age and location of residence to their buying patterns, including how much they spend, the frequency of their spend, and what they purchase.

Your customer database contains the valuable demographic and psychographic information necessary to define your target and communicate with them effectively. If you don't currently have a customer database, it's essential that you build one immediately. Without a customer database, you are missing out on opportunities to not only learn more about your customers, but also to zero in on targets for specific campaigns. To do so, there are several very good CRM tools available that will give you the structure you need to acquire, capture, and store pertinent data about your customers and prospects.

For instance, I used to be a longtime customer of a small jewelry store. The store was lovely and quaint, and the jeweler who owned it was an expert in the products he sold. But he didn't have a customer database. As such, he missed numerous opportunities to connect with current customers and existing prospects and grow his business. He could have easily sent direct response offers around holidays like Christmas, Mother's Day, birthdays, and Valentine's Day.

Personalized communication could have gone out to customers and their families as important dates, events, holidays, or anniversaries approached.

I spoke with this jeweler numerous times about the need for a database. I told him that, without it, he was missing the intrinsic value of his customers and missing important sales opportunities. That's exactly what any business that doesn't keep a customer database risks.

You can purchase lists that contain some of the targeting information you'd glean from a database, of course. You can buy a list sorted by any criteria imaginable—SIC code demographics, interest clubs, subscribers to magazines, association members, age groups, you name it. You can get these lists—thousands of mailing or email addresses—simply by going online. But using your own database of customers who have actually been to your business is of utmost value, and will be much more personalized and relevant to the recipient.

When you work from your own customer database, you can create all sorts of lists that you can then tailor a direct response marketing campaign around. Messages can be personalized based on recipients' purchase history, where they are in the sales funnel, and their familiarity with your business.

For example, imagine you own a lawn mower sales and service business. Assume most of your current customers reside in a specific zip code near your store. You decide to run three direct response marketing mail campaigns—one to existing customers who reside in that zip code, another to non-customers in the same zip code, and another to prospective customers who reside in other nearby zip codes.

Your message to them will be different depending on who the target is. In your message to your existing customers, you need to tailor your message and offer to acknowledge the history of doing business together before. If you know a customer bought a Toro mower from you last spring, you might send them a direct response marketing piece that makes reference to their previous purchase or the product they purchased. "Is your Toro Model XXXX in top condition for summer? Bring this coupon in by the end of March for a 10 percent discount on a complete service and a free blade sharpening."

Meanwhile, a prospect's message might contain more information about you and a more open-ended message pertaining to them: "Come in by the end of March for free blade sharpening on your current brand of lawn mower. Don't have a Toro? Here's an offer to bring in your current mower for service or trade in for a brand new Toro." You see how your message—and your offer—are different for customers versus prospects based on what you know about them, what they know about you, and their buying patterns and previous purchase history. You might even make reference to the most beautiful lawns in the area that are shaped by Toro and how their yard can look like those yards as well.

Data mining your customer database to personalize messages to your targets is really how you hit the bullseye with your marketing and grow your business. By tracking the frequency and types of transactions made by the customers in your database, you can identify, for instance, the top 20 percent of your customers by volume and target them with a specific campaign to increase their business frequency and spend.

Consider the example of a dry cleaning business. The owner might identify how often customers come to the cleaners and how much they spend. Do they come in once per month? Twice? Five times monthly? Do they spend $20 each time or $50?

By examining this data, the owner can then categorize the customers and tailor a direct response marketing campaign toward each category. The message to a customer that comes in four times a year is going to be different than a customer that comes in twice a year. You're aiming for the same thing with both customers—to increase their frequency and spend—but you'll use varying resources and different messages to do it.

You might invest a bit more on the customer that comes in four times a year, offering them incentives to boost their business frequency to monthly. You might turn that twice-per-year customer into a four-times-per-year customer with different offers. This is how you grow your business organically, by understanding the data and using it to identify your target and personalize your message and direct response call to action.

Merging Art and Science to Hit the Bullseye

Truly, direct response marketing is a science—based on data, facts, and numbers. It's also about the art of understanding the psychology of your customers so that you can communicate with them in the most compelling way possible. Recognizing and effectively reaching your target customer requires the use of both science and art. Studying your customer data to adequately target is the key to using direct response marketing to personalize messages that turn existing customers into more frequent visitors and prospects into customers.

When you do this, you're able to connect with a recipient—hit the bullseye—in a way most marketing methods can't. This in itself is unique and exciting. But what truly sets this method apart is the call to action. When you pair your personal message with a response mechanism, your message becomes results-generating.

It makes the next question a critical one: now that you have your target identified, what do you want them to do?

CHAPTER 6

WHAT DO YOU WANT THEM TO DO?

"He who conquers himself is the mightiest warrior."
—CONFUCIUS

Involve the reader in your copy.

The Five Ws of Establishing a Call to Action

By now, it's well understood that direct response marketing is unique in that it is designed to elicit an action from your prospect or customer. Once you have identified your target, your next step is to clearly define what it is you want them to do, and how you are going to get them to respond to your campaign. The action you ask of your target is critical because it's what is going to generate the desired results you expect from your campaign. It's what brings customers in the door and creates opportunities for you to do business.

There are several questions you can ask yourself as you set about creating this call to action, but there is one that stands out from the rest: *what do you want to accomplish? Exactly what result do you want?* Is it to make a sale, by getting the prospect to buy as a direct result of the message? Is it to start a conversation with a prospect? Is it to demonstrate something? Set an appointment? Do you want the prospect to call you, email you, go to your website, text you, fill out an information form, or visit your business?

There are myriad actions you could request. The point is to set your purpose. Too often, I see companies aim to just "send a mailer" without a clear, concise, easy to understand, and identifiable purpose. If you don't know, or you don't set predetermined expectations from your campaign, it will surely fall short. You must have clear, defined objectives for response rate, number of leads, appointments, or sales that you expect to generate as a result of your marketing investment in direct response.

So ask yourself: what do you expect to get out of this? At the end of the campaign, what will have to have happened for you to be completely satisfied with the result?

It helps to go back to basics when establishing your purpose by considering the five Ws of your campaign:

Who is your target? Who are you talking to? This takes us back to our discussion in Chapter 5—are they a customer or a prospect? What do you know about them that will drive how you tailor your call to action to them? You need to have a defined target; a defined "who."

What do you want them to do? What is the specific action you want your recipient to take? Bring in a letter? Bring their lawn mower in for servicing? Scan a QR code? A clear "what" is essential, and it will largely depend on who the target is because, just as in your messaging, your call to action for an existing customer who comes in monthly is going to be different than that for a new prospect.

Where do you want them to respond? Must they bring the letter they received into your business to redeem their free service? Attend a special event at the local fairgrounds? Call you to set up an appointment in their home? Visit a website? You must be specific about the exact location you intend to drive customers to in order to receive the response you seek.

When should they respond? Provide a timeline in which the customer must take the desired action. For example, is it a one-day sale? Do they have until the end of the month? Setting a time limit incites that concept we discussed previously—FOMO—and adds value to your proposition or offer. Your recipient must act within the time limit or they are going to miss out. Time-dated targeted messages are the most effective form of direct response marketing you can send. Establishing a timeline for your offer also helps you control when customers respond to ensure you have adequate resources to provide the best service, and it helps you measure the response rate for individual campaigns. Staggering the timelines of different campaigns gives clear visibility into which customers are responding to which campaign and simplifies the tracking of campaign success.

Why do you want them to respond? This calls back to our ultimate question: what are you looking to accomplish? This must be crystal clear because you'll only be satisfied with the campaign if your target does exactly what you want. And you can't expect that response or measure its success if you don't communicate that clearly. By specifying your "why," you can ensure the mailing you create is focused toward that goal. Also, be sure to be clear as to your "why" the prospect or customer should find value in your offer and act according to your request or call to action.

Answering these questions—fulfilling the five Ws—establishes control for you over the transaction with your customer. You define the parameters for who responds, when, and what they do. But it's important to remember who the recipient is exactly when crafting your call to action. At the end of the day, it's not about you, it's about them. There must be a reward in it for the recipient to respond to your request. A coupon, a discount, an offer. And whatever product or service you are offering, you must be solving a problem for the customer. If not, you can't expect them to have enough interest or desire to respond at all.

Placing Who, What, Where, When, Why: Goals for Success

Once you have established your five Ws, the next thing to do is specify how many responses you want to get from your campaign and target enough people to yield that response. The response rate you can expect is determined by who you mail to, what you say, what your offer is, and how many you mail. Other factors include the type of the mail piece sent, how personalized and targeted the message is to the prospect or customer, and the value proposition you are offering in your campaign.

Campaign responses can vary widely. There are a multitude of variables that can affect your response. The quality of your data, the creativity of the mail piece or message you send, and how compelling your offer is are all attributes that affect how many responders you will realize.

The timing of when the offer actually reaches the target also plays a role. For example, is the target in the market? Is your offer timed properly for the responder to respond on his timeframe? Are you allowing enough time for the responder to respond and realize the benefit of your product or service according to the wants and needs that it is attempting to satisfy? Does your timing make sense?

WHAT DO YOU WANT THEM TO DO?

Another huge factor is the quality of the offer. If your "deal" is not any better than a normal day of doing business with you, the recipient asks the valid question, "What is so special about this offer?" or "Why should I do this, when it is no different than any other day or any other competitor's offer?"

Another factor that affects response is how your message looks in the recipient's mailbox. If it looks cheap or inexpensive, it is likely to be perceived as such. Depending on factors such as the brand, the message, and the market, this can contribute to the number of responses you get.

One must always set a numeric goal for your campaign. If your goal is ten prospects responding, and you have a 1 percent expected response rate, then you know you need to mail to one thousand people to achieve the response you're after. The higher the expected response rate, the less you'll need to mail. You could set a goal of sales dollars, or possibly appointments set. Another goal might be inbound phone calls you receive as a result of your mail message.

Sometimes businesses seek responses in the form of website visits, text messages, or email replies as well. The response you expect is a function of the nature of your business and your particular sales funnel. Until you have some experience with your direct response messaging and test, and retest, and retest, you will not know what kind of response you can expect. I suggest you start off with a quantity you can handle, expect a 1 to 2 percent response, and then closely monitor your results to help you plan for future campaigns.

Get Your Target to Do What You Want Them to Do

Direct response marketing is all about eliciting a response from the customer. You need to know the who, what, when, where, and why of the response you seek. If you don't know exactly what you want the customer to do, you won't be able to measure the success of your campaign, and it will likely be less precise and targeted. Ultimately, you'll miss an opportunity to connect with customers and prospects and grow your business in a controlled and organic way.

Once you've done all this work—identified your target and established your call to action and response goals—you're ready to move on to the next step: putting together the best direct response marketing mail piece possible so you can meet (and exceed!) the goals you've set.

CHAPTER 7

PRESENTATION OF YOUR SELLING PROPOSITION

"People don't buy without a strong reason why."
—JIM EDWARDS

PRESENTATION OF YOUR SELLING PROPOSITION

Once you identify your most likely target and establish your call to action, it's time to create the most compelling, attention-grabbing direct response marketing message that will achieve the highest and best response possible from your customers and prospects. Particularly when it comes to direct response marketing via direct mail, the appearance of your mailing is a critical element as to whether it is read or trashed.

Personalization Is Key

The choices you make about the appearance of your direct mail piece should be rooted in what you know about your target. The direct mail targeted to someone who is a sophisticated investor or philanthropist will be distinctly different from a message being sent to a pet store prospect. The piece of direct response mail that is engaging a donor to make an annual contribution to a charity will be more than likely designed differently than one that is soliciting for a home air conditioner maintenance visit.

If you are a professional soliciting your clients, patients, or potential prospects who look very much like your clientele, you will want your mail to look professional. Use a high-quality envelope and highest quality stationery; maybe use embossed graphics, metallic finishes, and full color high quality printed inserts. Your offer should correspond to your prospect as well; it must resonate with the income, age, interest, and geographic characteristics of your current customers. After all, the look and feel of your mail should reflect the highest quality of the professional service or product you are marketing.

Someone targeting pet owners might not need to be as elaborate as the professional mentioned above. This marketer needs to focus on the type of customer or prospect who owns pets. What are their wants and needs, and how can that be conveyed with the materials you choose and by the creativity of how your message is conveyed?

Similarly, what you mail depends on several important variables. Because mail is tactile, the recipient spends time touching and looking at the mail, and much can be said about the sender by the impression the actual message extends to the target. Visually, high quality graphics, paper selection, color usage, font choice, type size, the clarity and lucid understandability of what your offer is, and what it is that you want the recipient to do are all factors that play into the effectiveness of your campaign, and ultimately the results you get.

Direct Mail Best Practices

While personalization based on what you know about your target is critical, there are some universal best practices and basic direct mail principles to consider as you create your campaign pieces.

Postcards, Flyers, and Envelopes

First and foremost, choices regarding the type of mailing and design must overcome the preconception that direct response mail equates to "junk mail." Of course we know this is inherently untrue—customer response rates and openness to marketing using mail proves that. But it's still important to elevate your campaign beyond the preconceived notions of junk by choosing the right materials and postage.

Often, postcards and flyers are viewed as junk because of their general nature. Because most postcards and flyers spell out the deal without any investment of time required by the recipient, the postcards and flyers usually are considered junk mail. Depending on how it is mailed, it may or may not be personalized, but because of the "open book" aspect of the ad, there is a dilution to the effectiveness of the offer or the offer simply jumps right out upon receiving the message. Because these formats are often less expensive and less complicated to send, the price you pay will be the cost of a perceived less expensive mail piece, which then devalues the offer and the brand.

That's not to say that postcards or flyers don't have a proper place for a direct mail direct response campaign. They can and very well do play a useful role in certain instances. When the sales message is on a postcard and it is already out front for the recipient to see, it is a quick touchpoint that hopefully will attract the attention of your buyer. Best of all, postcards and flyers are the most affordable direct mail marketing medium. You will usually pay more for a campaign sent using an envelope than you will via postcard.

Postcards can be designed with several different sizes, shapes, and materials to choose from. There are postcards that are 6 in. × 9 in. and 3 in. × 5 in. and 8½ in. × 11 in. We've sent flyers that are giant poster size, 3 ft. × 2 ft., printed on two sides that fold down to 8 ½ in. × 11 in. Fliers and postcards and even envelopes can be printed on heavy card or paper stock, glossy or flat, and these elements can make each campaign appear different. Postcards and flyers are often sent via standard postage, which saves the sender even more money.

However, it's been my experience after forty-two years in the industry that the benefits of an envelope far outweigh the cost savings that can be realized when using a postcard or flier. After running more than fifty-two thousand successful direct response marketing campaigns using direct mail, results prove that you can achieve a higher response rate when you send your message using a high impact or blind envelope. A high impact envelope hits the recipient with a very attention-getting or important-looking appearance. A blind envelope is one that does not reveal the sender anywhere on the outside of the envelope.

I am not a fan of printing your sales offer or unique selling proposition message on the envelope!

Nor do I like announcing who the mail is from, unless you already have a relationship with the target prospect. Offering a "free gift inside" or another proposition is often used and can work, but I really prefer capturing the attention of the prospect with uncertainty, more like, "What is this?" The more time investment a prospect spends with your message, the more likely you can convert the prospect to a customer.

Of course, there are tactics to avoid with enveloped direct mail pieces as well, such as disclosing information on the outside of the envelope. Some companies print what is referred to as "teaser copy," a message on the envelope hinting at what might be inside—something like "Get a low rate today!" or "Huge savings inside!"

I strongly advise against this. It gives too much away without requiring the recipient to open the envelope. The enveloped message might as well be a postcard or flyer. The piece becomes an advertisement, not a direct response piece. It undermines your message and basically wastes the envelope. You may as well pay the lower rate and send a postcard.

Meanwhile, if you receive an envelope with a logo of a brand you know, or best of all, nothing at all on the outside, the recipient won't know what it is. Is it money? Is it a bill? Information? Their interest is piqued because the envelope's contents are a mystery, increasing their likelihood of opening the envelope to at least see what's inside. The best way to send a direct response method via mail is in an envelope with as little information disclosed on the outside as possible. The objective of a direct mail direct response message is simply "Get the mail opened and read!" The main purpose of the envelope is to create curiosity, so that the more anonymity there is, the likelihood that it does get opened and read improves measurably.

Handwritten addresses and return addresses or envelopes with no return address at all are best, hands down. Laser printing capabilities today allow an envelope to be addressed in fonts that look remarkably similar to handwriting, so that's an option for marketers. Still, if and when hand addressing *is* possible, it's undoubtedly the best format to grab your recipients' attention.

Envelopes come in hundreds of different styles, sizes, printed or unprinted, coated or uncoated paper types, colors, windowed or non-windowed, and so each style needs to be best considered appropriate for your brand, your offer, your message, and your target prospect. Some envelopes are high impact, attention getting, that have the appearance of something urgent or important being delivered with a deliberate intention. Some are much softer, say a wedding announcement style-envelope, or possibly a greeting card-style envelope. Some effective envelopes are made to look more official or businesslike.

Rugged paper choices for your envelope construction, such as brown kraft paper, which is similar to the paper that is used by official or government-style envelopes, can give your mail message the appearance of something important that must not be overlooked. You can use envelopes that carry with them a likeness of a telegram, FedEx, Amazon, or UPS package. Several envelopes just use the street address and city, state, and zip for a return address, so the recipient does not know the source of the mail piece. Envelopes can be 9 in. × 12 in. or 6 in × 9 in., business envelopes (#10 or #7) with or without a window showing the recipient's name and address. Always be intentional about understanding what the envelope looks like in the mailbox when it is retrieved. Your objective is for it to stand out, look different, look important, look valuable, and look personalized. The envelope must beg to be opened!

Use First-Class Postage

There are several options when it comes to choosing postage and mailing methods. Understanding the differences can allow you to make the best choice for your campaign. It's important to remember that skimping on postage can diminish both your message and your recipients' response. It can also hinder the timing of your campaign. The postage choice says a lot about you, your company, and the importance of your sales message.

First-class mail. These are marketing pieces sent with a first-class postage stamp, metered first-class, or they have first-class indicia on them. There are several benefits to sending your mail first-class. First, this marking can give your mail piece a compelling appearance, demonstrating that priority was given to this communication (and, by extension, to the recipient). Second, first-class mail is promised by the USPS to arrive within one to three days from the postmarked date, giving you control over when your piece will be delivered to ensure it falls within the timeline of your campaign's requested response period. Finally, first-class mail will be forwarded if a recipient moves and leaves a forwarding address, and if the recipient did not leave a forwarding address, the U.S. Postmaster will return the mail to the sender, which enables the sender to cleanse and update his mailing list database. These features are not true of standard-class postage.

Presorted first-class mail. If you have five hundred or more customers or prospects that you're sending to in a zip code, then you may consider presorted first-class mail. This is when the mail is packaged and prepared before the mail carrier receives it. You get a better rate for presorted first-class mail than if you send regular first-class mail and the mail can still be forwarded. The postage says "presorted first-class."

Standard mail. Standard mail is what was previously referred to as bulk mail. It's less expensive than first-class, and it comes with pitfalls, including the fact that standard mail won't be forwarded to a forwarding address and delivery times can be longer and inconsistent, which makes it difficult to time-date a campaign or expected response. Quite frankly, the USPS does the best possible job they can do, but that said, standard mail gets delivered at the discretion of the postal carrier. Standard mail rates do save the mailer money, and the service is much improved over previous years, as most commercial mail is sent standard mail. There are several nuances that are required in the mail preparation, i.e. zip codes, carrier routes, number of pieces in a zip code, etc. but the savings can be substantial with volume and over time.

Mail sent via a special delivery carrier, such as FedEx. A piece sent via FedEx or UPS also provides a compelling appearance to recipients, and these deliveries clearly carry an air of importance. Additional benefits include the ability to track the package and exhibit more control over the timeline for delivery. These carriers are very expensive, but depending upon your product or service, your clientele, and your cost per acquisition, it may be the best investment you can make to acquire a new customer.

Additional Mailing Tactics and Considerations

There are other mail-specific marketing strategies and considerations that can boost your mail piece's appearance and increase the chances it gets read.

PRESENTATION OF YOUR SELLING PROPOSITION

Trojan Horse Letters

Trojan Horse letters present a direct response mail piece in a way that doesn't look like marketing. Named after the Trojan Horse in history, marketers use a similar tactic by sending a letter from a satisfied customer who wants to let a fellow consumer or neighbor know about a good deal they received from you. Whatever the approach, the Trojan Horse letter is intended to bypass any guards your recipient might have up by catching their attention with a non-traditional marketing piece and connecting it to your business via a call to action. The Trojan Horse method is when you have a third party, or what some people might call an influencer, write a letter to your prospect, endorsing you, your company, and your product or service. The envelope is personally addressed to the recipient and the return address comes from the endorser, not a business. The letter inside the envelope is exactly that, a personal note or letter from the endorser.

Lift Letters and Lift Notes

A lift letter is an additional letter or note enclosed within your mailing that is designed to "lift" your piece's visibility and, thus, your recipient's response. A lift letter is usually smaller than the main letter and it highlights the offer and the call to action. It is often personalized and is written by an influencer or someone other than the letter writer. We use 3M yellow sticky notes as lift notes, and provide a trackable phone number to set an appointment or place an order. They usually fall out separately and are easy to see and easy to read. Sometimes, the sticky note is applied to a folded-up faux newspaper clipping that references your product or service, or a note of endorsement or testimonial from a satisfied customer. The lift letter is sent *in addition to* and along with your original marketing piece solely for lifting response and reiterating the offer and the call to action in a short but powerful attention-getting note.

The lift letter is meant to encourage the recipient to read your sales letter, and it should be a smaller size or different color or paper type to set it apart from the main marketing material.

Dimensional Mail

You may have heard dimensional mail referred to as "lumpy mail." Simply put, this is mail that is three-dimensional rather than the standard flat mailing piece, and it can be very effective in reaching your target. Dimensional mail includes pieces sent in mailing tubes, boxes, or even bags. Items like game pieces, scratch and win game cards, scratch-offs, lucky number matches, puzzle pieces, keys, etc. all fall into this category. We used automobile ignition keys and placed them in cardboard tubes inviting prospects to come to a dealership and try their key in the ignition of the car on the showroom floor. If the key turned the ignition, the recipient was a winner. This tactic appeals to a customer's sense of touch by offering different textures and shapes. These mail pieces certainly stand out in a mailbox full of flat flyers and envelopes, making your piece feel significant to the recipient, which is interesting, and seeks to encourage them to open it.

Always check with postal authorities before you design your lumpy mail. You will need to get clearance and permission to mail these oddly sized messages, and there are several procedures that must be followed to meet USPS requirements. Lumpy mail is very effective, but it can be more expensive than all other forms of mailing direct response messages. Marketers must determine the ROI to justify whether or not it makes fiscal sense to use this form of marketing. We do direct response marketing for an artificial turf company, where we actually mail a sample square of the turf. We have mailed pizza boxes, videotapes, and several other unusual containers for both B2B and B2C clients that demand attention.

Keep Paper Size and Texture Fresh and Targeted

The paper size and texture of your direct response mail piece should depend largely on your target and the response you're soliciting. If your target is a financial client to whom you wish to sell a financial portfolio, for example, you need a format that appears elegant and professional. Highest quality cotton or linen stationery might be considered.

There are dozens of formats and sizes to choose from. I recommend constantly changing up the look and size of your pieces so they're not predictable for repeat recipients. If a potential customer receives a similar looking package in the mail frequently, it could decrease your response rate because they've seen it before and know the contents. Making campaign pieces look different each time piques your prospect's interest and curiosity, allowing your message and your brand to remain fresh to them.

Colors and Fonts Really Do Matter

Regardless of your target, the most important part of your direct response marketing piece—the message—must be clear, legible, and easy to read, which means choices like which font and what size are important. Serif fonts are always a good choice because they appear neat and clean. Use fonts that correlate to the recipient. For example, if your message is targeting seniors, it is wise to consider a font size that is somewhat larger than what you might normally use. Also, make sure that your copy is easy to read. Long, tight leaded copy is difficult to read, and you might lose your prospect before they get the entire thrust of your offer.

Carefully chosen colors in your design can also help your mail piece stand out from the rest of a recipient's mail. Experts[30] report that certain colors can evoke specific emotions in a recipient—for example, red conveys excitement and passion; blue portrays feelings of harmony and peace; and yellow invokes optimism and positivity. Bright colors may coincide with faster responses. Consider the emotions you want to evoke through your campaign and design accordingly. Use colors that complement each other and keep in mind balance and white space to create an eye-catching and pleasing piece.

Keep Your Mailing Professional and Personalized

Considerations of paper size, font, texture, and postage may all sound simple and common sense, but don't be fooled—these decisions are

---

[30] Summer Gould, "11 Shades of Direct Mail Strategy," BrandUnited, accessed April 18, 2023, https://www.brandunited.com/article/11-shades-of-direct-mail-color-strategy/.

actually quite complex. They comprise the art of direct response marketing. All of this requires some serious thought: *How are you going to reach your customer? What is going to spark their curiosity enough to open your mail item, take the time to read it, and then complete the action you're asking of them? You need to remember to "just talk to them." Your message needs to be as if you were speaking to your neighbor across the fence.*

These tips, knowing your customer, and knowing precisely what you want your prospect or customer to do will enable you to create a visually appealing, attention-getting piece of direct response mail that will elicit the action you seek. Without a professional and personalized appearance, your prospect might discount the importance of the sales message or offer you are presenting. And the message, of course, is the most important part of all in developing your campaign. What you say and how you present it is instrumental in not only reaching your target but also maximizing their response.

CHAPTER 8

CRAFTING YOUR MESSAGE

"Make it simple. Make it memorable. Make it inviting. Make it fun."

—LEO BURNETT

It is all about them. Not you.

CRAFTING YOUR MESSAGE

If there's one piece of advice I can offer you when developing a direct response marketing campaign, it's this: *the secret to success is in your messaging—what you say and how you say it.* Start with the results you expect and work backwards.

This is to say that, while everything we've discussed up to this point is important, your target's response largely hinges upon the content of your message and how it's written. This is how you will make your piece stand out from all the other marketing messages your potential customers receive. It's what makes your campaign work. Truly, it all comes down to what you put in the letter.

It is important to remember always, when crafting your message, you are selling. This is markedly different from advertising. This message is on a mission, and that mission is to get an order, a purchase, a call, an appointment, a visit. Remember you are selling an idea, not necessarily selling your product or service. Of course your product or service has benefits, features, and advantages that will be included, but your true mission is to elicit a response by tapping into the human emotions of the reader.

First and foremost, you must speak to your prospect or customer, just as how they would like to or expect to be spoken to. Your direct response message gets into the home when the salesman can't. Therefore, it needs to be personal in that the message needs to be written as if you were talking to a close friend or even a family member, sitting across the kitchen table from them, or in the case of a business message, as if you were sitting across the conference room table or sitting in their office.

The best way I can illustrate this point is with a case study. We once did a campaign for a client who owned an RV service company. We identified his list of most likely prospects and best customers—existing RV owners in a geographical area in close proximity to his service center—and then sent them a simple postcard that illustrated a family dealing with a broken-down RV. There the family stood, stranded in the middle of what looked like a desert, clearly stressed because the RV that was supposed to be transporting them on their summer adventure was broken down on the highway in the middle of nowhere.

The image was accompanied with a message that read something like: "Is your RV ready for your summer vacation? Before you head out on vacation, be sure to bring your vehicle in so we can check it over for you. You don't want this to be you." We offered the customers discounted service on their RV if it was brought in during a certain timeframe in the months leading up to summer.

The campaign was immensely successful at bringing the business's existing customers in, as well as reaching and gaining new first-time customers. The service center realized a 1,100 percent ROI and increased their service business by 50 percent while the campaign was in effect all thanks to a well-thought-out message and value offer.

Articulate the Problem

If we dissect this piece of mail a bit further we can see why the messaging worked so well for my client and how following similar best practices can work for your campaign, as well.

To begin, we did something every direct response marketing campaign piece must do: *we articulated the target's problem*. We put the recipient in a vacation mindset, then presented the biggest problem they could encounter during it—their RV breaking down in the middle of the desert. What would they do if this happened to them? They'd be stuck. They'd have to spend time and money getting their RV towed and staying in a hotel while it was fixed. The entire vacation they had waited all winter for would be derailed. It compelled them to do something about this now so this unfortunate circumstance wouldn't happen to them. We appealed to the emotion of fear of loss to suggest getting their RV maintenance check.

Regardless of what you're selling or trying to get your target to do, articulating your target's problem is where you want to start. Sometimes, you're articulating a problem your target didn't even know they had—perhaps these customers hadn't even thought about getting their RV serviced to prevent a breakdown. Either way, your marketing piece should bring that potential problem to light.

A key to keeping your messaging fresh is seasonality. What problem are your customers facing right now? Whether it pertains to holiday gift giving, preparing for vacation, readying for cold weather, or anything else, articulating a problem allows you to do two things: keep your messaging fresh with each piece you send, and create a sense of urgency in dealing with the problem. You might say, "Service your home air conditioning system now before the hot summer months leave you baking in a sauna," for example. Or, "Scan this QR code for free shipping and guaranteed delivery before Christmas." Or more popular today, "Scan this code and shop our inventory before you come in."

I personally send monthly letters to my customers, and each time, I present a current problem the dealer may be facing at the time. For my car dealership clients, for example, January is often a slow month, so the copy speaks to slow showroom traffic, quiet winter nights, and bulging inventory that must be merchandised. Of course the simple, safe, and affordable solution I offer is a direct mail campaign that will drive buyers into their showrooms, and get phone calls, emails, and web hits.

Whatever the problem is—and whether your customers are aware of it or not—when your target audience reads your communication, they should think, "Oh, wow. That's precisely my experience!" Hitting the nail on the head is always the goal when articulating a problem in your message.

Promise Your Solution

Once we articulated our RV customers' problem in our direct response marketing piece, the next step was to offer the best solution possible to motivate customers and new prospects to act: come into our shop before summer and we'll check your RV for you, and if you come in during the program period, you can get our top-notch service directors at a discount.

The key to this is formulating your unique selling proposition (USP) and making that clear to your recipient. What are your product or service's benefits, features, and advantages? Promise them a solution to their problem. Catch your readers' attention by promising them a benefit. Call it out in the headline, elaborate on it in the subhead, and then expand further in your opening. Showing your readers what's in it for them is the only surefire way to grab attention. Why is your solution the best one to solve your customer's problem?

It's critical that you say the right things and present them in the right way to elicit a response. With that in mind, consider the following additional tips when creating your message.

Your Offer

A unique or special offer or incentive is the best way to get customers to act. Make one or more offers per mailing, and make it something that will prompt direct and immediate action. A time dated invitation or coupon for a discount, for example, inspires a prospect to take care of an issue now, rather than later. And we gave them a time limit, so Urgency was built in to generate a measurable response as well as a prompt to suggest to the customer he must Act Now!

Always keep the customer at the forefront of any solution you offer. What will the customer get if they reach out to you? It should never be about you as the seller or your business. It's for this reason that I'm always baffled when I see realtors mailing flyers with pictures of a house they just sold. What good does that actually do for the prospects? How is it useful to them in solving their problem of getting their house sold or buying a new house?

Of course, most realtors want to get listings, and by showing a photo of a house that they just sold, they think that anyone who is thinking of listing their house will give them a call. More important are the facts surrounding the sale—facts such as number of days the house was on the market, if the seller was able to get their asking price, the time to close the transaction, and how many homes they have sold in the past three months. Including a relevant offer is the best way to help a customer solve their problem—and in doing so, it sets your message apart and inspires your recipient to act.

One alternative might be for the realtor to send a message telling them that they have buyers interested in the prospect's home. Since the market is so explosive, now is a good time to consider selling your home, and as a top realtor in your area, the realtor might describe how confident they are to be able to get them top dollar for their home. Always try to help your readers imagine themselves enjoying the benefit or outcome you've promised. This approach appeals to your prospects' emotional triggers. Specifically, elaborate on how your product or service will make this benefit a reality.

Back up the picture you've painted for your prospect with cold, hard facts: statistics, research studies, charts, graphs, testimonials, expert certifications, product photos, and even product demonstrations will improve response. Always be sure to illustrate just how much value your recipient will receive. Your goal is to link the promised benefit to the enticing picture to the acceptance of the proof…

all to result in your prospect or customer taking the desired action that you want them to take.

Use Power Words and Phrases to Get Attention

The key in crafting your message is to keep it simple. People don't want to get bogged down with big words or long complicated copy. Grab their attention with short, pithy, common, easy to understand language that will be relevant and will resonate with your target audience. Avoid long paragraphs. Always make sure your sentences are flowing as if you were speaking directly to your reader.

We know that "free" is the most powerful word you can use in marketing, and one of the best ways to drive the highest response rate possible is to pair your call to action with a free gift.

"Free gift," "send no money," "guarantee," "easy," and "risk-free" are all powerful, attention-grabbing phrases. Most importantly, they will eliminate any perceived risk in responding to your message. Whatever you do, always consider articulating how you can minimize risk. Your message must communicate that responding is easy, saves time or money, and that the recipient has nothing to lose by reaching out and pursuing the action you're requesting. You can minimize risk by offering terms, or lengthening the time to pay.

Include powerful words like enjoy, try, capture, own, take, grab, seize, and have. The best copy consists of a series of short and powerful statements. Good copy exudes benefits to the recipient and is laced with supportive information that debunks any doubt the reader might have about the offer. Good copy will even address objections head-on, to eliminate any doubt the prospect might have about you, your company, or your product or service. Copy that includes testimonials and supportive graphs and data is also an extremely effective way to back up your promise of a problem's solution. Any reference to the exclusivity of the prospect, customer, offer, or time limit will enhance response rates.

Be Straightforward and Conversational

When it comes to tone, the key to reaching your customer is to write to them like you're having a one-on-one conversation with your prospect. Keep it conversational, personal, sincere, and honest. Prospects can detect insincerity and false promise if it is served up. Keep it simple. Most people are busy, and your message needs to get directly to the point in simple terms. Always write about them. Talk to them about them. Refrain as best you can from talking about you. Always write about them, their health, their lives, their home, their car, their children, their pets, their future, their retirement, their ambitions, their fears, worries, etc.

It is not about you. It's all about them. Write like you are talking to your neighbor, especially if you are familiar with your customers. All of your previous customers want to feel special, so talk to them because they are special, regardless of whether you have a personal relationship or not; cautiously and respectfully speak to them as if you do. They will appreciate it. After all, they've done business with you, spent their hard-earned money with you; they are the lifeblood of your business, so speak to them conveying how important they are to you and your business. If you are writing to a prospect, or someone who you do not yet have a previous business relationship with, your copy needs to acknowledge that fact, and your message must recognize that you do not yet have the relationship you intend to develop with the prospect.

That is personalization. Always know exactly who the message is being directed to and speak from that vantage point. If you have different classifications of your list, i.e., customers and prospects, then your copy should be different for each, and the message for each needs to be specific to each recipient.

The Parts of the Letter

How does one go about constructing a sales letter that will articulate the problem, offer a solution, and keep all of the best practices we've discussed in mind? Let's deconstruct the specific parts of your message to gain a better understanding.

The goal of direct response marketing, or more specifically, direct mail, is to elicit *action*.

It is like an opera of sorts. A four-part approach to getting the prospect or customer to take action. First, get attention. Second, create interest. Third, provoke desire. Last, move the recipient to take the action you want. Give them a reason to act, and act now!

Every direct response sales letter will include three specific parts—the salutation or the Johnson Box, the body, and the sign-off. There are specific aspects to keep in mind for each of these to achieve the highest response rate possible.

Salutation

The very first words your recipient reads in your message can have a big impact on your results. The most important word there is to any person, anywhere, at any time, is their name. Therefore, the most important word that you must integrate into your copy is the customer or prospect's name. You can start the sales message or flyer or postcard copy off with the customer's name. You can then integrate their name throughout the copy in the appropriate places. There are some established examples you've likely seen on direct mail pieces you've received: "Dear neighbor," "Dear investor," "Dear fellow pet owner," the list goes on. Usually, the more specific and personal you can be, the better. That is why I highly recommend you address your prospect by name.

Of course, just as with hand-addressed envelopes, personalization comes at the cost of time and money. Many programs are available where variable data can be inserted into copy during the electronic printing process at a reasonable cost. Therefore, the most important thing to remember in your salutation is to be friendly and personable when greeting your recipient.

Sometimes direct marketers use what is called a Johnson Box, that is, basically a headline, conveying the problem or the solution to an existing problem. Either way it is front and center, and attention-getting from the get-go summarizing the problem or the solution your sales message is proposing. Writing from the customer's standpoint, your goal is to involve the reader in the headline. Engage them here. Your prospect or customer is interested only in themselves, not your product or service. They are not interested in things, but only what things can do for them! Your headline sublimates the story; it tells the essence of the story you are going to tell. And you must appeal to your prospect on their own terms. "Can't sleep?" "Play better golf," "Is your dog healthy and happy?" Get the best possible benefit of your product or service to stand out clearly in your headline.

The Body

Once you've greeted your recipient, you want to grab their attention and keep them reading. There are several approaches to do this. Posing a simple, compelling question is one effective way to draw them in. Examples of opening phrases I've used on previous campaigns include, "Will you try this experiment?" "Could you use an extra $500 per week?" "Can you do me a favor?" "Will you try this test?" "When was the last time you…?" "Did you know that?" "Are you curious about…?" "Do you ever ask yourself the question…?" "Are you paying too much for…?" "How can you cut the high cost of…?" "What is the most effective way to…?" "Remember the first time you…?" and hundreds more. Curiosity is a very strong factor in human nature. You can spike interest using curiosity.

Telling a story is always an effective approach. Examples include: "I want to tell you about my friend, Ann, who for years suffered from numerous health problems," or, "I was chatting with my neighbor about investments the other day, and he told me he had a few thousand dollars spare cash, but he had no idea where to invest it." This approach shows you understand and can relate to the customer's problem—it accomplishes that putting-your-finger-on-it requirement of articulating the problem.

Talk benefits. Promise benefits. Because benefits whet desire. Appeal to curiosity. Be sure you write with enthusiasm. If you are not enthusiastic, neither will your reader be. Try to use words that wake up dozing minds. Your copy needs to ring a bell or blow a whistle.

You can appeal to pride or incorporate human interest. Distinguish your offer from others by expounding on the benefits. Benefits are the advantages or the satisfaction that one will receive. People only buy to get benefits, but the benefits must be supported by clearly delineated product points. Such benefits could be comfort, pride of possession, more time or less time, money saving, better health, improved fitness, better sleep, etc. Write to illuminate to the reader in as quick and complete a way as possible for him/her to perceive what would it mean to them to take the action, or possess, enjoy, or live with the product or service you offer.

People also buy for the negative benefits as well. Negative benefits are instances where loss is avoided, disadvantages are avoided, income loss is avoided, or safety is ensured. Tell the customer or prospect how your product or service will improve his or her life. Advertising speaks to features; direct response copy addresses how the reader will benefit from the most important features of your product or service. Make sure you promise the benefit.

Another approach is to open with a statement that tells the recipient they are part of an elite or specially selected group chosen for this special promotion. This provides a sense of personal interaction and being chosen or singled out for a deal others can't obtain. Examples of these statements include:

- "You are among a very small group of [grill owners, gym members, homeowners, for example] invited to use the gift certificate we have enclosed."
- "The enclosed gift certificate is being sent to a very select group of customers and is available for a limited time."
- "Our records show that you are one of our best customers. We want you to be among the first to take advantage of this new offer."
- "You've been selected."
- " Your name has appeared on our select list of _____ _____."
- "This is your personal invitation…"

The one thing you must always remember is that you are not only selling your product or service. You are selling human response to human emotion. Human nature. You are selling whatever it is that appeals to people. What emotion can you tap into? Fear? Fear of loss? Safety? Security? Pride? Love? Gain? Duty? Responsibility? Self-indulgence or self-preservation?

The more motives you can appeal to, the more successful you will be. Here is where you need to tie your product or service to love, fear, hate, pride, greed, freedom, vanity, or hope and find an emotional connection and amplify it. Good copy will draw on the emotional needs of your reader. The desire for money, love, respect, and self-improvement are some of the strongest emotions I've seen from responders. Show your prospect how you can help them meet those needs. The more emotions you can tap into, the better the response will be. Tie your product or service to what people want at their core, and you will be able to connect emotionally much more easily. It is through this emotional connection that you will incite your prospects to take your desired action. People buy on emotion and justify it with logic. The greatest motivators are fear and desire. What really gets people to act is "What they feel."

After grabbing the recipient's attention, it's time to tell them your solution—state your USP. Tell your customer how your business, product, or service stands out from the competition, and how they stand to benefit from it. Explaining your product or service's USP helps build your message into your call to action. When making your offer, make sure that you are outlining a convincing reason Why you are making this incredible offer. It must be a true reason, and it must sound convincing. Examples like: "The season is nearing its end, and we are overstocked with units left over."

Or possibly a convincing statement like, "The factory has over-shipped this inventory to us, and we must sell these units to make room for…"

Another tactic is to use a selling sentence. The most common selling sentence all of us have heard every time you walk into a McDonald's is, "Would you like fries with that order?" It is a compelling sentence or two that gets to the heart of your offer, and it is proven in almost any circumstance where selling your "deal" takes place. The message leaves the reader almost unconscious of the message, because he is so enthralled and interested in the action you want him to take.

Keep your recipients reading by using compelling transitional words and phrases. Connectors like, "So, what does this all mean for you?" "This is not just my opinion," and "Does this sound familiar?" all keep recipients engaged with your message so they can get to the most important part of all—the offer and the call to action. The best way to make this transition is to use the magic words, "which means…"

For example, "(feature)… Which means… (benefit)…," "Which means you will be able…," "Which means you can…," "Which means you will enjoy…," "Which means you won't have to…," "Which means it will not…"

Remember to remind your recipient that there is no risk in redeeming your offer. Some examples of ways to communicate this include:

- "Send no money, and if after fourteen days you decide not to keep the [product] or continue the [service], cancel with no questions asked."
- If you decide to cancel your subscription to [service], I want you to keep the [gift], valued at [gift value], as our way of saying thank you for giving us a try."
- "You can't lose. Any risk is ours. This is a win-win for you."
- "If you decide to keep [product], we will bill you in four monthly installments. That's just a total of [amount] a day,

less than your average cup of coffee. But if you don't like it, simply cancel or return it to us and you pay nothing."
- "Unconditional money-back guarantee!"
- "You must be 100 percent satisfied. If not, we will give you a 100 percent refund."
- "You won't find this guarantee anywhere else!"
- "Free trial offer!"

The body of the copy is where you tell of the features and advantages: you place the most emphasis on the benefits of your product, service, event, sale offer, special deal, etc. This is where you tell your story of what it is that the recipient will realize by accepting your offer and taking the appropriate action you are asking of them. This is the copy that sells, just as if you were selling face to face. Be sure that you give them good reasons to do what it is you want them to do. Answer any questions that might come to their minds while reading this copy and face any objections they might have head-on. This is the meat of the message and should be leading the prospect or customer further and further toward taking action.

Point out what the customer will gain by taking action and what the customer will lose by not taking the desired action. Help your reader imagine themselves enjoying the benefits or the results you are promising to them. Emphasize how the product or service will make the benefit a reality.

Your message needs to make the reader want what you have to offer, not for what it is, but rather for what it will do for them. You can distinguish your offer by pointing out several exclusive features of your product, service, or offer. Illustrate a favorable comparison to another product or competitor. Contrast superiority with exceptional claims and convincing support of the benefits of your product or service. Why is it better? What exclusive features make it better, or what was done to make it so? It is effective to use testimonials and tell of the popularity of the product or service.

Sometimes, great copy includes quotes or an authority's endorsement. Testimonials, cold hard facts, statistics, research studies, third-party reviews, product demos, or photos help you provide the proof you need to support the image you have created. Powerful copy always gives assurances, provides a guarantee, or overcomes any objections a reader might have. Give your reader a good reason to act or to purchase from you. Be sure your copy is selling you and your product or service, and for you alone, not anyone else who might be selling a similar product or service. You have a better location, a better selection, a better sales team, or an exclusive offer not found anywhere else!

Lastly, make the choice to take action easy and tell them *now* is the time to act. And most importantly, ask for the order! People need to be asked to do something, to take action, or to buy. Make a bid for action by issuing an invitation and by tying a major benefit to taking action *now*! First, clearly state your call to action. Simply including your company's phone number and website isn't enough. You must be explicit and clear about what you want your recipients to do. Examples include:

- "We'll let you be the judge: scan here to receive your free trial right now and get ready to change your life!"
- "Don't delay: bring your discount voucher in today for service at a reduced price."
- "Mail us this voucher to send you a trial issue as a free gift and let us wow you."
- " I urge you to act at once."
- "_____ is just a phone call, text, or email away."
- "Learn more about this at www._____ or by calling _____."
- "Take advantage of this offer by just _____ _____."
- " Now is the best time to _____ _____."
- "Get started immediately…"
- "This is a time-dated offer, time is running out."

Use words and phrases here that convey excitement, hope, and urgency around your offer. Some examples include "amazing," "exclusive," "reduced," "immediately," "remarkable," and "limited-time offer." More powerful words are "shocking," "spicy," "riveting," "outrageous," "earthshaking," and "jaw-dropping." There are several resources for words to express attention getting and that elicit an emotional response.

Finally, close your communication with a memorable sign-off; finish your mailing with a warm, personal, and friendly end. "Sincerely, "warm regards," and "respectfully yours" are classic examples. If immediate action is desired, a closing like, "We await your answer" adds a bit more urgency in the request for a response.

Regardless, here is where you reiterate your Risk Free offer. Your offer of a guarantee will help move the prospect to take the action you want, if the need and the desire have been established.

Sign-Off or P.S.

Finally, close your communication with a memorable sign-off.

The use of a P.S. has been proven to be one of the most effective ways to summarize or communicate the crux of your offer. Some experts extol that the P.S. is the first bit of copy even read when the recipient opens the letter. Readers scan to the sign-off to see who it is who is writing the letter and will then drop to the P.S. to get the last message, which usually reiterates the main point of the body of the letter, and it also repeats the call to action.

- P. S. Want to save *even more?*
- P. S. There is more!
- P. S. Did you know that…
- P. S. Remember.…
- P. S. If you act now…
- P.S. To claim your free gift…

Experts also suggest that the writer title is not one of marketing or sales because then the readers understand it is purely a sales letter.

The main thrust of the copy of the letter is best when it speaks to providing an easy and affordable solution, or when it solves a problem and is offering helpful information.

Create the Best Message to Reach Your Target Effectively

The tone and content of your message is the secret to success in direct response marketing. What you say all depends on what you want your customer or prospect to do in order to take advantage of the solution you are offering. How you say it impacts your ability to elicit that response. You must win his confidence, and earn his or her belief in your statements. It starts with understanding and articulating your recipient's problem, then offering the best value and easy time-saving, money-saving solution possible to solve that problem. Most importantly, since direct response is selling, your message needs to definitively ask for the order.

As a side note, when the best copywriters write copy for direct response, all the rules of traditional writing go out the window. Use Capital Letters in the Middle of your Sentences to get the effect of speaking directly to your prospect. **USE BOLD COPY.** Use *italics*. Stop and start your sentences with thoughts, blurbs, and key points. Use etc. etc… Incorporate exclamation marks! (parenthesis) and underline for emphasis. Double space. Indent. Use bullets.

All of these techniques will help you get your message to the reader and excite them to take action. Remember, you are not writing a college paper that a professor will scrutinize. This is a conversation.

You are talking directly to your recipient., so write like you talk. Talk with emphasis. With drama. With pause…all the while keeping it as simple as possible. So it is understandable. Easy to read. Easy to follow along. Easy to engage. Easy for the reader to feel the copy as it resonates with her.

And as best you can, make it fun!

When you communicate your sales message in an accessible, simple, yet conversational way, you will be personalizing your message and reaching your target in a way few other marketing methods can. It's talking directly to your customer or prospective customer without any inhibition or formality. It's why direct response marketing is so effective. And we know it's effective because we are able to quantify our results and track response and sales, which leads us to the most important metric for measuring success: return on your investment, or ROI.

BE DIRECT

CREATIVE SOLUTION PROCESS

WHO? → WHO IS THE TARGET PROSPECT? → WHO ARE CURRENT CUSTOMERS?

WHAT? → WHAT DO WE KNOW ABOUT THE TARGET PROSPECT? → WHAT IS THE OFFER? → WHAT BENEFIT(S) WILL THE PROSPECT REALIZE? → WHAT IS THE DESIRED ACTION? → WHAT IS THE MAIL PIECE?

WHEN? → WHEN DO WE WANT THE PROSPECT TO RESPOND? → WHEN IS THE OFFER IN EFFECT? → WHEN DOES THE OFFER EXPIRE?

WHERE? → WHERE ARE THE BEST PROSPECTS? → WHERE DO WE WANT PROSPECTS TO GO TO RESPOND?

WHY? → WHY SHOULD THE PROSPECT RESPOND? → WHY WILL PROSPECTS TAKE THE DESIRED ACTION?

CHAPTER 9

ROI—THE GOAL OF DIRECT RESPONSE MARKETING

"The only purpose of advertising is to make sales. It is profitable or unprofitable according to its actual sales."
—CLAUDE HOPKINS

The Ultimate goal of any business is to make a profit. You are in business to get results.

ROI—THE GOAL OF DIRECT RESPONSE MARKETING

ROI, OR RETURN ON INVESTMENT, OR PROFIT, IS THE GOAL of any enterprise. If you cater to any other aspect, you might soon find yourself discredited. And as the decision-maker of your company's marketing budget, you're likely thinking about advertising or marketing ROI day in and day out. You need to know that you're spending your marketing dollars wisely. You need to know your strategy is yielding a return on your investment and you are getting the results that you set out to get. There are many money pits, or what I call "black holes," where hard-earned funds can be deployed for advertising and marketing your product or service.

If you are not closely monitoring your spend and the results you are realizing as a result of that spend, you are not doing your job.

Of course, you know that's easier said than done for most marketing methods. As we've discussed, traditional advertising and digital marketing methods, such as radio, TV, newspaper, SEO, PPC, and retargeting, are difficult to accurately track to measure your return.

That's the beauty of direct response marketing. No other marketing method allows you to so easily and quantifiably track ROI while simultaneously gathering useful data so you can make the best decisions for your future marketing spend.

Calculating ROI with Direct Response Marketing

When you sit down to establish a new strategy or assess your current marketing strategy, it is important to consider the expected ROI. *Are your advertising and marketing efforts reaching the right people? Are those contacts—or impressions—turning into sales of your product or service? Are you making a profit? How many leads or interested prospects were acquired? How many conversions were converted to sales revenue? What was your profit per sale? What was your cost per lead? What was your closing ratio? And a multitude of other metrics that will determine the effectiveness and the value realized from your spend.*

You may have analyzed numbers for some of your current marketing campaigns and found that ROI number to be fuzzy. You can't say with complete certainty that a sale can be attributed to a specific ad or campaign. You don't know exactly how much revenue was the result of a specific promotion.

With direct response marketing, that calculation of ROI is clear and straightforward, which makes it an extremely valuable tool for any marketing professional. You can easily track the cost of the campaign. You know exactly who and how many targets you targeted, how many replies or responses or orders you realized, and the profit made from the sales made to those targets. You will want to know your response rate, your conversion rate, your sales generated, your gross profit generated, your cost per lead, and even your closing ratio. Learn more about which marketing piece pulled best, who responded, where the responders reside, how much each order basket yielded, which customers spent the most, which products were purchased, etc. etc.

ROI—THE GOAL OF DIRECT RESPONSE MARKETING

In a business world where you may be overloaded with data about site visitors, click-through rates, ad impressions, and more, direct mail makes it refreshingly simple to see exactly what your marketing spend is bringing in for your company.

We've already talked about how direct response marketing is both an art and a science, and this is the science part of the equation. Simple math with direct response marketing gives you so much valuable information.

You will know that you targeted X prospects with your campaign with this specific offer. X recipients responded to the offer—you know because you requested a very specific action from them that indicates they are responding to this particular campaign. This is best measured by the response vehicle (i.e. coupon, discount, phone calls, web hits, emails, text messages, showroom floor visits, or a sales offer that is unique to your campaign) utilized during a specific time frame. Therefore, you can calculate how many recipients converted into closed sales. The actual number of sales and gross profit generated from the campaign is your *return*.

From there, you already know how much you spent on the campaign or your investment. How much did it cost you to get those customers to buy your product or service? Now, take your profit dollars and divide by the amount you spent on the campaign. That is your ROI. You should get greater than 100 percent return every time. For example, if you spent $5,000 and you realized $5,000 in gross profit, you realized a 100 percent ROI or the campaign generated enough profit to pay for the campaign.

That's good, but not what we are after. We seek returns of 300 percent, 500 percent, 1,000 percent, or 10X your investment. Note: I still might argue that 100 percent return is an excellent response.

I have argued that even in the event that no one responds to your campaign, you still realized your money's worth. When compared to all other advertising media where measuring ROI is possible, the medium of direct response outpaces all of them because with most all other forms of marketing and advertising, you never can be precisely sure as to what it was that moved the customer. Your brand, your message, your product or service was introduced into the home or office of your prospect, and if your campaign was executed properly, it was a prospect who has a high propensity to buy your product or service. How does that match up to a radio ad that goes to the entire market, or to people who have no interest at all in your business, product, or service? You are at least reaching the right people at the right time with a compelling message that will resonate with the recipient at the appropriate time in the buying cycle.

Direct response marketing gives you all of the data that you need to track your campaign, measure your success, and help you make informed decisions about where to allocate your marketing dollars toward future marketing initiatives. You can examine exactly who responds, where the responders are coming from geographically or from which list selection or data mine, and what were identifiable characteristics of those responders who took the necessary action. These are critical facts that you will want to uncover to enable you to make informed decisions going forward. You might even dig deeper and explore which responders generated the most sales and most revenue or highest profit per transaction. When you know this, you will seek prospects who look like those responders. From where geographically did you get the best response and most resulting sales? And many more tailored metrics to satisfy any chief marketing officer, CFO, or CEO.

You Can Control Budget and ROI with Direct Response Marketing

The ability to precisely measure ROI provides another distinct advantage for marketers using direct response marketing: control.

Direct response marketing, particularly through direct mail, allows you to keep your costs in line by sending only what your marketing and advertising budget can afford. Rather than a monthly fee, as you are required to do when purchasing SEO services, for example, you can send ten letters a day or ten thousand, depending on what your budget allows.

Not only can you control and spread out your investment, but you can also control and spread out the return. I've run campaigns for businesses in which we've mailed letters indicating that recipients should bring the included coupon in on a specific day. We mail 5,000 letters listing a specific date, and fifty customers come in on that date. We mail 5,000 more listing a different date, and the dealership gets fifty new customers coming in on a different day. It allows for steady business and a steady return.

Testing and Tracking

With so much control over what you send and when, direct response marketing enables marketing executives to also test and track their marketing efforts to optimize for effectiveness and enhance ROI. In fact, this is something you should always be doing—trying new approaches to discover, learn more, and understand what works. Test, test, test!

As we have discussed earlier, several variables within a direct response marketing piece can impact the response. The format of your mailing, such as letter versus postcard, for example, can play a huge role in a mailing's response rate. The appearance of the package, the tone and content of your copy, the structure of your call to action, and your specified response mechanism are all grounds for tracking and testing to determine which gets the best results.

You might find that a mailing asking for a phone call elicits a stronger response with certain customers, while a QR code response mechanism is more effective for another subset of customers or offers. This information helps narrow down and tailor approaches to best reach your targets and helps with future decision-making when shaping campaigns.

For example, I worked on a campaign for a company that helps doctors process their denied insurance claims. To test our approach for maximum effectiveness, we mailed some doctors a postcard, while other doctors received a letter in an envelope. Both subsets of the target received the same message, but it was presented in different ways. Then, we evaluated how effective the letter versus the postcard was by tracking the response rate so we could decide which format to use going forward.

Just like you should be constantly changing up elements of your mailing to keep it fresh for your targets, you should also constantly try new ways of connecting with your targets. Change your copy or the response mechanism; try a new offer; package the mailing differently. Then, compare the results. It's incredibly interesting and empowering to be able to track and test your marketing with such precision and control, and then make intelligent marketing decisions based on that data.

Even When It Fails, Direct Response Marketing Wins

One final benefit of direct response marketing that's really unmatched in most other methods is that, even if your campaign does not elicit a strong response at first, it still does several things for your brand and marketing strategy. The multidimensionality of direct response marketing means that, regardless of the response rate for your campaign piece, it still makes an impression, just like a billboard or a newspaper ad or a sign on the side of a bus.

Plus, you have gained information you can't always get from other methods. You can test and track and analyze what works for certain targets in a way that other advertising methods can't provide. That is invaluable to the marketing professional trying to bring in more sales, revenue, profits, and market penetration.

Consistency often breeds results in direct response marketing. A campaign might not "work" the first time, but when you keep going—when you keep tracking and testing and measuring and analyzing—you start to see how it really *does* work. It starts by making an impression, and then, as you tailor and tweak your approach, you're able to use that valuable information to maximize your ROI. It's art and science working together, which is exciting. The possibilities are endless.

ROI = Success

As a marketing executive, I don't need to tell you how essential ROI and the ability to measure it is to your job and the success of your company. It's the purpose of your marketing strategy, what it's all about.

Undoubtedly, direct response marketing is a highly reliable way of tracking ROI, particularly when executed through direct mail. But in today's business environment, we know that direct mail isn't the only medium for marketing for most companies. The world is digital, and if you're like most organizations, success in your industry requires an online presence.

The good news is, you can leverage digital marketing channels to execute the best practices and principles we've discussed thus far. Digital integration with direct response marketing is possible—and necessary—to grow your business.

CHAPTER 10

DIGITAL INTEGRATION: USING DIGITAL CHANNELS IN DIRECT RESPONSE MARKETING

"The secret of all effective advertising is not the creation of new and tricky words and pictures, but one of putting familiar words and pictures into new relationships."

—LEO BURNETT

Allow customers and prospects to live vicariously with the product or service.

DIGITAL INTEGRATION

First off, all businesses need to be advertising online; technology has launched marketing into a new era, and digital is at the forefront. So among the plethora of digital applications and media options available, you will likely choose several different digital methods to pursue and await the results.

Let's say that your digital contract renewals are approaching and you're faced with evaluating how that particular digital strategy has paid off. The problem is, you can't quite pinpoint exactly what you got for your investment. The results are often underwhelming. Click-through and open rates on the email campaign are relative key performance indicators, but what was your conversion to sales ratio? Did your recipients even see your digital sends? You've been advised that your social media ads and SEO efforts should be directly and clearly attributed to sales—that they led to a lot of website visitors and impressions, yes, but you can't definitively say they led to conversions.

If you can relate to this scenario, you're not alone. Many companies use digital channels to advertise and find themselves in this same predicament. It's because they're relying *solely* on digital marketing to reach their customers and bring in sales.

What most marketing directors don't recognize is that, in an effort to optimize digital marketing results, it's possible to apply direct response marketing principles within them. By integrating digital approaches and direct response marketing, you'll find the two approaches work harmoniously to modernize your marketing strategy while bringing you the customers, sales, and ROI you need and expect.

The Benefits of Direct Response and Digital Marketing Integration

Integrating direct response and digital marketing means taking the direct response marketing principles we've discussed throughout this book—the same processes of identifying your target and asking them to do something—and then using digital tools to elicit that response. Rather than a recipient bringing in a coupon for 20 percent off their next purchase (or a free quote or service, or whatever the case may be), they are prompted to obtain their offer digitally.

This can be accomplished in a variety of ways. You might send a direct mail piece that contains a QR code leading to a microsite. Recipients can scan the code and then visit the site to make their purchase, get a quote, request more information, pre-qualify for credit, or schedule their appointment. You could prompt recipients of your direct response marketing piece to email a specific address, visit a URL to watch a video, call or text a specific trackable number to obtain their offer.

It sounds simple enough. But in my experience, integrating these two approaches into one strategy isn't done nearly enough. When it is, several benefits can be realized.

Enhance Your Response Rate

Many times, implementing direct response marketing via digital channels increases your response rate for the simple reason that it's easier for recipients to respond. No longer do they need to leave their house and bring the coupon into the store. Instead, they can scan a code and buy online, send an email or visit a website to schedule an appointment, text, call, or chat, all on their own time from their own device. Less effort is required on their part, which often increases the likelihood of response and improves your campaign's results. Risk is reduced, because control of the outcome is now placed in the hands of the prospect.

The goal of direct response is to identify a handraiser, or an interested prospect or buyer. All of these tools described allows the sender or marketer to capture this information, and even in some cases begin an ongoing conversation with the prospect about the product or service. Some marketers email, text, or even call responders immediately in real time once a prospect has identified themselves.

All digital ads, including Facebook, Instagram, and Pinterest, can include a direct response mechanism. A simple call to action that identifies the source of the ad will help you measure your response and conversion and sales rate.

Track and Measure ROI

Integrating direct response and digital also enhances your ability to track responses and measure ROI. Personalized URLs and microsites can be set up for individual campaigns, making it easy to identify which recipients and how many recipients of a direct response marketing piece visited the site. Website destinations for scanning QR codes or campaign-specific phone numbers can also be established for ease of tracking. Similarly, unique email addresses and text addresses can be created to receive emails and texts elicited from a campaign. All of this works to identify respondents as coming only from that marketing effort, which allows you to track your responses, attribute conversions to specific campaigns, and measure profit and, thus, allows you to calculate your ROI.

Glean Customer Information

Trackability of direct response in the digital sphere extends beyond measuring ROI. These personalized digital tracking mechanisms can also be used to glean information about prospects and customers who make purchases.

Each time a prospect who you target with mail responds to a direct response piece, there is information about that prospect that is known. Just by scanning a QR code or visiting a website, you have an opportunity to learn who that prospect is and obtain any data, such as the prospect's name, address, phone number, and all other pertinent information you already have attached to that record. This process also affords you the opportunity to seek any information you want from them once they arrive at the destination microsite developed for your particular business or campaign.

For example, you might send a mailer with the *action* message, "If you'd like more information about this money-saving technique, scan here for a free report." The recipient may scan the QR code, which takes them to a microsite with a form to register for the free report. It's prepopulated with what you already know about the prospect, but then it could ask them additional questions that you might want to know, that simultaneously drives them further down the sales funnel. By completing the registration or information request, you can then retarget this prospect based upon the important and relevant information they share with you.

Now, the prospect has obtained their free report, and you've not only obtained valuable information for future correspondence, but also identified that prospect as a "handraiser"—someone who you know is interested in what you are selling and closer to conversion.

You can now more accurately target these individuals with your future marketing efforts. The next time you send a direct mail piece or email asking prospects to view a video or visit a website to make a purchase, you won't be sending the link out to just anybody—you'll be sending it to handraisers who have an expressed interest in you, your company, your product, or the service you offer.

Pull Prospects into the Sales Funnel

By identifying a handraiser, you do something very important for your business: you draw a prospect further into the sales funnel. You take them a step closer to transitioning from a prospect to a customer. Out of all the people targeted, these people have identified themselves as live prospects for whatever product or service you're marketing to them.

Now you can go back to those people and ask for the sale. Perhaps a prospect is identified as a handraiser by sending an email to acquire a discount coupon, but then they didn't visit your store or business to use it. Now that you have qualifying information and know more about them, this allows you to follow up to say, "Hey, you haven't been in to use your discount. Your offer will expire on said date. Be sure to take advantage of this special offer before the expiration date. Call us if you have questions about this unusual offer. Can we set an appointment for you? Do you have any questions?"

Even the mere act of using a digital response mechanism, rather than an in-person action, immediately brings prospects further into the sales funnel. The ability for recipients to take action—make an appointment or buy a product, for example—from their device increases the likelihood of conversion versus having to physically visit your place of business to redeem their offer.

Leveraging Tech for More Conversions

Technology such as chatbots can also assist marketers with leading prospects down the sales funnel by doing things like having a fact-finding session to further qualify the prospect or scheduling appointments. Chatbots are interactive chat technology platforms that can interact with users on their phones or computers. Essentially, the automated dialogue takes the first steps in leading your prospects further down the sales funnel, freeing up you and your sales team to focus on those who are at or closer to the decision point to make the investment in your product or service.

In my business, we regularly use chatbots for auto dealerships with great success. Here's how it works: the recipient scans a QR code on a mail piece to visit a microsite that prepopulates the microsite form with everything we know about that prospect—data like name, address, phone number, type of car they drive, and the last record of the car's mileage.

The chatbot then confirms this data is correct: "Is this correct? Click yes or no." If any data is incorrect, the chatbot prompts the visitor to correct it via questions: "How much are your monthly car payments?" "How many payments do you have left?" or "How many miles are on your car?"

With this new data, the chatbot then leads the prospect further toward the answer they seek—that is, down the sales funnel to doing business with our client dealership.

The chatbot might ask if the prospect is interested in trading in, and then ask a series of questions to identify the exact type of new car they want, right down to the exact make and model.

Then, the chatbot does the most important part of this whole process: it makes it simple and easy for the prospect to make an appointment at the dealership. The bot might say, "To give you the best amount for your trade-in, we would like to take a look at your vehicle. Would it be possible to bring that vehicle into the dealership?"

When the prospect responds, "Yes," the chatbot gives the prospect a calendar with scheduling options, allowing them to choose the appointment slot that works best for them. It then ends the conversation with a confirmation of the day and time of the appointment and a summary of the information, which also goes directly to the sales team at the dealership in real time to prepare them for the appointment and to add to their customer database. It also triggers an email confirmation to the prospect.

You can see how, by using digital technology, the dealership has now moved from a traditional direct mail letter asking the prospect to visit or call the dealership, to automatically moving the prospect into the sales funnel by actually setting the appointment.

This chatbot technology can be used for any type of business, from setting appointments for a chiropractor, dentist, or eye doctor, or for reservations at a restaurant, to purchasing products online, or home maintenance requests for heating and air conditioning, plumbing, gutter cleaning, lawn service, or extermination service.

Digital Marketing + Direct Response = Maximum Effectiveness

You may be asking how pairing digital with direct response helps with the disappointing digital marketing results you've received thus far.

My answer is twofold. First, pairing digital marketing and direct response provides you the trackability to constantly test your approaches to see what works. Rather than throwing money at several different digital tactics, but never being able to truly measure your success, using direct response principles within your digital marketing strategy allows you to track response and ROI and compare such approaches to optimize your results. It's how you determine whether you put your marketing dollars toward social, PPC, or SEO, targeted digital or retargeted digital, email or text message marketing. It gives you the data you need to make an informed decision.

Second, integrating direct response marketing principles into your digital marketing approach allows you to overcome a major downfall of digital on its own: that you don't really know where your message is going.

We know that social media is awash with fake or fraudulent accounts. In 2019, Facebook removed more than two billion fake accounts in a two-month timespan.[31] This means that running a Facebook ad without a way to reliably track who is clicking and responding to it makes it difficult to justify the expense. A Juniper research study from Q1 2022 reported that the value of digital ad spend lost to fraud will reach $68 billion globally in 2022.[32]

According to some industry experts, there will be up to $23 billion in ad fraud losses in the U.S. just in 2022.[33]

We also know that a large majority of email ends up in spam if a customer does not already have a relationship with the sender. Paying for an email campaign can be the equivalent of throwing money out the window. There's a good chance your recipients may never even see it in their inbox.

The advantage of direct mail over email is overwhelming. When you apply U.S. postage to your message, you have the guarantee of

---

[31] Kaya Yurieff, "Facebook Removed 2.2. Billion Fake Accounts in Three Months," CNN Business, last updated May 23, 2019, https://www.cnn.com/2019/05/23/tech/facebook-transparency-report/index.html.

[32] "Top Five Ad Fraud Hotspots to Watch in 2022" (whitepaper, Juniper Research, 2022), https://www.juniperresearch.com/whitepapers/top-five-ad-fraud-hotspots-to-watch-in-2022.

[33] Scarlett Woodford, *Digital Advertising Fraud* (Juniper Research, 2022), https://www.juniperresearch.com/researchstore/innovation-disruption/digital-advertising-fraud-research-report.

the United States Government that your message will be delivered. Of course, the recipient may choose to discard your message, but you did get your money's worth; the ad message or letter was in fact delivered to the targeted and desired prospect. With email, it is much different. Yes, you send the email. You might even send it to the most desirable prospect or even your customer database. However, it remains up to Google to determine whether or not your email reaches your target recipient. If you don't believe me, take a look at your spam folder. You will be surprised by the brands and names you know, who you may have even done business with or purchased items or services from, who sent you paid messages that you never even knew came to your inbox. That is the most distinguishing difference between what is considered email or digital marketing and traditional direct response. Yes, email costs less, but you truly do get what you pay for.

These are the downfalls of using digital advertising on its own. Sure, it's where your customers are and so it's where you want to be, but it's not nearly as effective at reaching your target or turning your prospects into customers.

Of course, the same can be said about using direct response marketing via direct mail on its own, as well. Today's world revolves around cell phones and computers. Our society is transfixed by technology. For most companies, that means digital marketing strategies are essential. Relying solely on direct mail could be a strategy for the right businesses, but I suggest it be used in tandem with other forms of ad media for utmost effectiveness.

Thus, the sweet spot for maximum effectiveness is when direct response principles are used to complement digital channels. Direct response marketing is trackable and quantifiable; you can see who responded to your call to action on that Facebook ad. Or you can establish a relationship via a direct mail piece first, then follow up with an email campaign to your active customers, making it more likely your email will land in the customer's inbox rather than their spam folders. Pairing direct response marketing with digital channels harnesses the best of the digital world, and increases your chances of not wasting your money on anything fraudulent or untrackable.

Don't Miss Your Opportunity

For most marketers, the motivation to move their advertising strategy to a digital platform is the same: your customers are on their digital devices and their phones, so you need to be there, too. There is no doubt that your company needs to have a digital presence.

What is often overlooked, however, is that digital advertising can be paired with direct response marketing principles. Otherwise, it could be a missed opportunity to target more effectively, learn more about your customers, track ROI, and move your prospects further into the sales funnel. Using direct response principles in combination with digital marketing channels not only introduces modern technology into your approach, but it also improves your strategy—and, with it, your results.

CONCLUSION

I'll conclude this book by challenging you with a task:

Put this book down and go out to your postal mailbox. Go ahead. Put it down. I'll wait.

Did you retrieve your mail? What did you receive?

If you're like most Americans, your mailbox was full with offers. Credit card offers from American Express, Citibank, Capital One, Barclays, Bank of America, and Wells Fargo; letters from GEICO or State Farm Insurance asking you to switch your home or car insurance for a lower rate; deals on new internet or TV packages from telecommunications giants like Spectrum and AT&T; maybe even smartphone advertisements from a huge company like Verizon. National Chains use mail like Target, Bed Bath & Beyond, Costco, Walmart, and National Grocery Store chains, and more. Even Google and LinkedIn use mail in a B2B context. Catalogs, postcards, letters, invitations, marriage mail, and more.

These offers aren't just coming from the mom-and-pop shops down the street. These are *huge* companies. Successful companies. Public companies with massive marketing budgets.

Why—when these companies have the money to employ any advertising tactic imaginable—do they employ direct response and direct mail on a national scale?

Because it is effective. Because it works!

Don't think nobody has informed these marketing professionals at these major companies that the strategy of direct response does not work; that they haven't heard that the method of reaching their best customers and prospects is outdated; that people don't open their mail; that monies directed toward direct response marketing should be reappropriated to SEO, PPC, Facebook, or Instagram.

These high-powered professionals in these high-paying positions have likely heard all of that, and yet, they know the return on their investment they get with mail makes sense for them to continue it.

Truthfully, it is the best-kept secret in marketing. You are reaching customers and prospects with a stealth strategy, since your competition cannot truly evaluate the breadth of the reach of the campaign, that is, even if they ever discover your strategy. And, once again, you got your important sales message or offer in the home or hands of the right target. Now that's value!

It's all because direct response marketing works. It works because it's personalized, it's trackable, and it's based on solid data about prospects and customers. And in today's digital world, there are very few methods that offer those benefits. It makes it worth considering as part of your marketing strategy to fuel your company's success. Direct Response is essential in complementing your multichannel, integrated marketing initiatives.

CONCLUSION

Why Direct Response Marketing Works

As you know, one of my aims in initiating this conversation about direct response marketing was to dispel the myths about it. These myths include that direct response marketing is dead, direct mail is junk, and that no one opens mail anymore in today's digital age.

There's no better way to devalue those statements than to prove how effective direct response marketing can be, which is exactly what we've done. Let's revisit the reasons direct response marketing is one of the most effective—yet overlooked—marketing methods available today.

It's Personalized

Direct response works because it is a personal medium.

Direct response marketing allows you to target, drill down, and segment prospects and customers in a way that's just not possible with most other advertising methods. Personalized direct messaging means you can nurture existing customer relationships and establish new ones with potential prospects, to keep the lifeblood of your business strong.

It's Measurable

Direct response methods allow you to track who responded to your campaign and who didn't; what worked and what didn't; and how much you spent to bring those customers into your sales funnel. When it comes to making decisions about your marketing budget, there's nothing more valuable than trackability and measuring ROI.

It Puts You, the Marketer, in Control

When you establish the communication, the offer, and the response mechanism, you control how your customers respond, when they respond to your promotional event or sale, and when they engage with your business. You can spread out your ROI, work within your daily, weekly, monthly, or yearly budget, and ensure you are always able to provide the best products and services that will keep customers coming back.

It's Visible

When a person receives a direct response communication by direct mail, it is a tactile piece of marketing information that gets into the home or office and has substance. Prospects may see it and decide they aren't interested and throw it away, but they make that decision. Consumers like it because it allows them to be in control. They can read it, set it aside for later, or toss it. Maybe even keep it handy for when they are ready to be in the market for what your company is offering. It's not automatically filtered to a spam folder by Google, or it's not just one of another hundred digital advertisements seen by your prospect in a given day. In today's digital world, that visibility is tremendously valuable in and of itself. Truthfully, if the prospect is in the market for your product or service at that particular point in time, or has any intention to be, it will be difficult to argue that the prospect will discard or disregard your marketing message anyway.

CONCLUSION

It's Relevant

The more time consumers spend at home, the more their personal USPS mailbox is an effective way to reach them. This trend makes direct response marketing via direct mail more relevant and embraced by more consumers, both young and old, than ever before.

It Identifies the Handraisers

Clearly put, direct response marketing makes it simple and easy to identify prospects who are interested in what you're selling, which allows you to target and communicate more effectively, more frequently, more predictably, and more relevantly—and to ultimately result in bringing in more sales.

This fact is the crux of why direct response marketing works. I've seen it with my own eyes. If you send someone a reasonable offer for something that they're in the market for at that moment, you cannot convince me they won't respond to it. You also cannot convince me that the people who respond are not interested. All the people who weren't interested either tossed that piece of direct mail away or didn't respond to it. The people who did respond are at least somewhat interested—they are the handraisers, and they are now in the sales funnel.

These respondents are not cold leads. They are people who know what you're selling, know what your pitch is, know something about your product, and are interested in buying. Otherwise, they wouldn't be responding to the offer. That's the beauty of direct response marketing and the essence of its effectiveness. It self-identifies prospects as they become closer to actually making a purchase. And, most importantly, they responded when we asked them to, as opposed to the prospect who enters the sales funnel when they choose to do so at their volition.

It's all about sales and making a sale. Sales professionals know that they have to have control of the sales process when making a sale. When a responder responds to your offer, you have established the first line of offense, because you have established control of the process.

Science, Art, and Possibility

I already told you that I am not an all-knowing marketing guru. What I am is a very seasoned professional, with more than four decades of experience in direct response marketing under my belt. And as one professional speaking to another, I will reiterate this point: direct response marketing works. *I guarantee it!*

As you stare down at your latest marketing report and wonder: *What should I do? Where do I invest this hard-earned money? How do I reach our best customers? How do I bring in more traffic, more sales? How do I prove that I am getting an acceptable ROI?* I encourage you to do what I prompted you to do at the very beginning of this book: ask yourself *what if?*

What if you considered this number-one secret weapon in marketing for boosting response, retaining your customers, acquiring new customers, getting leads for your sales force, and seeing immediate traffic and sales as a result?

CONCLUSION

What if you applied all the principles we discussed in this book to your next marketing campaign? What if you took those digital advertisements with underwhelming results and applied direct response principles to them? What if you gave some serious thought to what a direct mail marketing piece might look like, in reaching out to your customers or potentially new customers who look like your current customers?

In every one of the fifty-two-thousand plus direct response marketing campaigns I've conducted since I started this company, the principles covered in this book—from the science of the data to the art of the messaging—were applied with great attention to detail. And I humbly tell you, they returned great successes.

If you have not considered direct response marketing for your business, it might be a good time to do so. You're equipped with the knowledge, you understand the principles. Now is the time to maximize your ROI, glean valuable information about your prospects and customers, and increase your brand's visibility in a way you have never done before.

Good luck and good selling!

ACKNOWLEDGMENTS

I must begin by thanking my mother and my father for their love, care, guidance, and direction while I was growing up and for their emphasis on the importance of education. I will be forever grateful for their teaching me the value of hard work and commitment and an untold number of life lessons.

This book would never have been possible without having started my company forty-three years ago. That monumental event would never have occurred without the encouragement I needed at the time that was so generously given to me by Marty Paligraf and the unconditional support to "go for it" that I received from Cindi Paligraf, Rick and Cindy Kushner, and Steve and Jill Ochsner.

There are a few incredibly special individuals who trusted in me and who believed in the efficacy of direct response in the very beginning. I owe heartfelt thanks to Bruce DeBona and Anna Jarrnigan, who were my first two employees.

My passion for direct response was recognized first by trusted clients Keith Mason and Jim Weldon, and my company was essentially built on the foundation of their support. Early believers were the Dallas–Fort Worth Area Ford dealers and Rich Arb and Mike Duffy at the Ford Division of the Ford Motor Company, who literally put us on the national map.

I am indebted to Alan and Stefanie Goldstein and Dan, Doug, and David Baum, who have been my advocates for forty-three years.

The treasures expounded in this writing were realized by some of the biggest names in the automobile industry. I can never express enough gratitude for all that has been given to me by both clients and best friends Ron Pietrafesso, J.R. Malouff, and Chuck Fairbanks.

They rode this ride with me from the beginning. Industry icons Larry H. Miller, Doug Spedding, Ron Carpenter, Billy Fuccillo, Brian Benstock, Sam Pack, Jay Cimino, and Dean Fitzpatrick have contributed and have realized huge benefits from the principles expressed here.

Credit for this book goes to the entire Larry H. Miller organization, Hud Romero, Ernie Riach, Dave Montemorano, Phil Peccoraro, Todd Hilleboe, Bill Stahlein, and Cory Naneman, who consistently worked with me in the development of new and exciting direct response programs.

I am grateful for all the support I received from Jim Click and Sam Kayhat, Ed Garrett and the John Elway Dealerships, AutoNation, Joe Sheridan and the Sheehy Dealerships, Ed and Steve Snyder, Jerry Reynolds, Charlie Nixon, Randall Reed, Mike Lowrey, Rick Foley and Paul Bozant, Jack Herrin, Tommy Harvey, Bob Guenther, Alan Lukehardt, Jon Anderson, Bob Boyte, Bob Tiso, Randy Fuergeson, Randall Noe and Randy Lee, Milton Killebrew, Charlie Tubbs and DC, Ken Zangara, Russ Darrow, Don and Sherri Herring, Gene Osborn, Mike Nohr, Rich Gray, Joe Tigue, Mike Surrey, and Leo Griggs.

ACKNOWLEDGMENTS

Praise and thanks to Jim Carrol, Phil Bonfonti, Geri Opera and Lisa Landis, John Shock, Ann Pollack, John Byrd, Gary Dilts, Tom Marinelli, John Kramer, Mike Grammes, Tim Morrison, Mike D'Amato, Nick Verna, Phil Scroggin, Steve Bland, Steve Wagner, Derrick Todd, and Paul Hofelich for the confidence they placed in my ability to assist them in driving the response they needed for their dealers.

I am grateful for Jori Sheldon and Spencer Beckstead at Saxton-Horne, John Giovatto, Dennis Flaherty, Jason Matt, and the ad and marketing teams at Giovatto Advertising, Saatchi and Saatchi, JWT, TBWA Chiat-Day, Y&R, GM R-Works, Cramer-Krasselt, and the Southwest, Northeast, and West Business Centers of Chrysler, which is now Stellantis. Special appreciation to Ken Frisbie at Tax Ease and Mike Molina at RVDA.

Most of what is written in this book is the result of what has been learned from the tireless contributions made by the incredible team members over the years at TACITO DIRECT, especially Gerard Luisi, Andy Munro, Dang Nguyen, John Sauber, Sandra Cobb, Faye Elmer, Ray Vo, Binh Vuong, Danielle Ledat, Loretta Reed, Rex Vardeman, Narry Balakrishnan, Madison McCalib, Scott Songulay, Dana Biggs, and Tina Nolan. A special tribute goes out to Tom and Judith Harris, Terry McMillan, Travis Thrall, Denise Smith, David Morton, Steve Cochran, Karl Farmer, Kelly Gavagan, Terry Robison, Carl Mock, Dorthy Gosset, Jennifer Shaw, Patti Bosco, Mignon Scott, Susan Gray, Dean Tilden, Megan Matthews, Marcia Paulas, and Caroline Binz.

Without their dedication and commitment to the work we were doing, none of this could have ever happened. I appreciate you all, and thank you again.

I want to thank my friend and mentor, Claude Giroux, who has been my north star for thirty-three years.

I wish to acknowledge all of those clients not mentioned above who were both users and benefactors of the principles of direct response marketing.

Lastly and most importantly, this book would not be possible without the inspiration, guidance, and direction keeping me on course by my copilots, Jennifer Byrne, Sophie May, and the entire team at Scribe.

Milton Keynes UK
Ingram Content Group UK Ltd.
UKHW020119030823
426179UK00015B/241/J